Making Ends Meet

Making Ends Meet

Farm Women's Work in Manitoba

Charlotte van de Vorst

UNIVERSITY OF MANITOBA PRESS

University of Manitoba Press
Winnipeg, Manitoba R3T 2N2 Canada
www.umanitoba.ca/uofmpress
Printed in Canada on acid-free paper by Friesens.

Cover Design: Karen Armstrong
Text Design: Sharon Caseburg
Cover photographs courtesy Provincial Archives of Manitoba, Jessop Collection.

National Library of Canada Cataloguing in Publication Data

National Library of Canada Cataloguing in Publication Data

Vorst, Charlotte van de, 1959-
  Making ends meet : farm women's work in Manitoba / Charlotte van de Vorst.

  Includes bibliographical references.
  ISBN 0-88755-667-1

  1. Women in agriculture--Manitoba--History. 2. Rural women--Employment--Manitoba--History. 3. Rural women--Manitoba--Social conditions. 4. Farmers' spouses--Manitoba--History. 5. Agriculture--Economic aspects--Manitoba--History. 6. Sexual division of labor--Manitoba--History. I. Title.

HD6077.2.C32M36 2002   331.4'83'097127   C2002-911374-1

The University of Manitoba Press gratefully acknowledges the financial support for its publication program provided by the Government of Canada through the Book Publishing Industry Development Program (BPIDP); the Canada Council for the Arts; the Manitoba Arts Council; and the Manitoba Department of Culture, Heritage and Tourism.

Contents

Introduction

Far too little is known about farm women the world over. With this in mind, I began a study of the history of women's economic contributions to the family farm in Manitoba, as part of the requirements for a Master of Arts degree in Anthropology. To document not only what work farm women did in the past, but how and why it has changed, I consulted censuses and other government statistics, local community histories, and general histories. I soon discovered that there was very little historical documentation of farm women's work in these sources. Censuses, for example, do not consider housework as an occupation and women who do this work on the farm are excluded from census figures. In addition, women who work both on and off the farm and who report their off-farm job as their occupation find their farm-labour contribution excluded from census figures. Local histories suffer from similar shortcomings. Family accounts, for example, generally trace the male line only. Women are assumed in their father's and husband's identities or are mentioned in passing as wives, mothers, and daughters. Local histories also tend to associate certain milestones, such as the first homesteads, crops, and roads, with pioneer men. General historical works on Manitoba, too, are dominated by a male perspective, which largely excludes the role of women in the province's agricultural history. The terms "pioneer," "settler," "homesteader," and "farmer," for example, are attributed implicitly to the male gender. What is more, descriptions of farming routines tend to focus on commercial activities undertaken by men only. Women's work in food preservation, dairying, cloth manufacture, and farm operation are not mentioned. The participation of women in activities conventionally thought of as men's work is ignored as well. This, for instance, is the case with reaping grain and haying. Moreover, descriptions of technology usually focus on tools handled by men; the walking-plough or threshing machine are mentioned, the spinning-wheel and scrubbing board are not.

A major reason why historical sources do not tell the story of women's work is that they have relegated the work of women to the household, which is viewed as being unrelated to crop and livestock production. This misconception reflects society's perception of gender roles in general. Housewives, for example, are commonly viewed as non-workers because their work does not take place in the marketplace. In addition, the household is seen as having lost its productive function—as being exclusively a unit of consumption—since it is assumed that economic production in the home has been taken over by industry and that major services like health care and education have been institutionalized. The advent of labour-saving devices, too, is considered to have reduced women's work in the home. However, as the growing number of academic and non-academic studies on women's work show, housewives produce a multitude of goods and services not provided by service industries and social institutions. They produce the meals, the healthy children and well-fed adults, as well as the clean living quarters, without which the rest of society could not function. The economic importance of housework becomes apparent when one considers how family members would cope without the services of homemakers: they would have less energy and time to devote to work for pay in the marketplace.

Nowhere is the economic interdependence of men's and women's work more obvious than on the farm. With women taking care of family needs, men can be freed to work in commercial field-crop and livestock production. This link between men's and women's work is even more apparent during periods of economic crisis. For example, it is commonly believed that family standards of living depend solely on the income earned by family members working in the market place, usually the male 'breadwinner.' It is assumed, then, that when family income drops or inflation outstrips wage increases, the family automatically suffers a reduction in well-being. The fact that housewives work harder to maintain the same standard of living is overlooked. They buy fewer processed foods, make and mend clothes more often, put more effort into bargain hunting, and postpone the purchase of appliances. In doing so, they function as a buffer against the initial shock of an economic crisis. This is particularly evident in Manitoba's farm history. Each time the wheat economy failed and farm income dropped, women, as the title of the book indicates, made ends meet by economizing on expenditures and, moreover, by generating extra income through a variety of economic pursuits. They milked more cows, expanded their gardens, and increased their poultry flocks, which not only provided their families and hired hands with the basic necessities of life without drawing on farm income, but also provided a surplus for market, which enabled them to purchase needed family items not produced on the farm. In many cases, women's income from these sources was the mainstay in the first years of settlement and continued to be important in marginal areas where income from wheat remained limited. Although the 'wheat cheque' may have financed the bulk of farm improvements in prosperous years, women's economizing activities and their income from the sale of butter, cream, poultry products, vegetables, and country provisions provided the family and the farm with the material means critical to survival when grain prices were depressed. Consequently, farm women always have and still do contribute to the economy of their farms in many direct and indirect ways. Indirectly, they economize and earn extra money for household expenses so as not to divert farm income away from farm improvement. Directly, they work on the land and with the livestock and invest their, sometimes considerable, excess income in farm assets.

In this book, I have set out to document the history of women's work on Manitoba farms. It is founded on the comments and observations of 130 farm women and men, whom I interviewed across the province between 1985 and 1988. Their stories, as well as the autobiographies and published archival accounts of numerous pioneers, provide a more balanced overview of farm women's work, how and why it has changed, and how it interrelated with the work of their husbands. The book is divided in four chapters, each dealing with a specific period since Red River Settlement days. Women's work on the farm is described against the background of larger social and economic circumstances. The first chapter describes how economic isolation, coupled with slow, manual methods of farming, limited farm families in the Red River Settlement and on the frontier to subsistence production and demanded a high degree of task sharing between men and women on the farmstead. The following chapter describes how men's and women's work became more segregrated in response to the technological innovations in farming and housework, as well as to the coming of the transnational railway, which set the stage for commercial agriculture in the province. The next chapter documents the economic importance of women's economizing and income-generating activities on the farm. It also shows the interrelatedness and complementary nature of men's and women's work on the farm. The last chapter describes the changes in farm women's work in more recent decades, starting with the boom in agriculture following the Second World War and ending with the crisis of the 1980s.

This book is a step in acknowledging the full contribution of farm women to agricultural development in Manitoba—a contribution which has been subject to a high degree of understatement. In documenting Manitoba farm women's work, it joins other recent studies in helping to fill a void. I hope that farm women can identify with it.

1.
Era of Subsistence Farming

Women's Work on Red River Settlement Farms

Before 1870, when Manitoba became a province of Canada, settlement in western Canada was slow. The Red River Settlement, established in 1811, was home to predominantly Scottish, French Canadian, and Métis farm families living along the banks of the Red River, between Pembina and Lower Fort Garry, and along the banks of the Assiniboine, between Upper Fort Garry and Portage la Prairie. The farmland was located on long, narrow river lots. Winnipeg was a village of 215 inhabitants. Except for the occasional sale of farm produce to the Hudson's Bay Company or private fur traders, there were no domestic markets. To the Hudson's Bay Company, which owned and governed all of western Canada east of the Rockies, agriculture in the Red River Settlement existed merely to support the fur trade, the company's main economic interest. Without railways, export markets were also non-existent.

Economic isolation, coupled with slow, manual methods of farming, limited Red River families to farming for family use. This subsistence production was very diverse, combining livestock and poultry keeping, dairying, gardening, and cereal cropping, with the manufacturing of unavailable items, all of which provided for life's necessities. An average family of six kept two or three horses, eight or nine head of cattle, two sheep, four pigs, and several chickens. Subsistence gardening included a wide range of vegetables. Reports of the mid-1800s indicate that commonly used table vegetables such as turnips, beets, cabbage, asparagus, broccoli, shallots, onions, and potatoes were of good quality and grown in quantity. Melons and pumpkins were also raised. Wheat, barley, and oats were common field crops. Some settlers planted dwarf Indian corn as well, "especially," as historian W.L. Morton put it, "where Indian blood ran in the veins of the farmer."[1]

Wheat was used for making bannock, scones, and dark, hard loaves of bread. Oats and barley were important as livestock feed. The Scots also used oats for making oatcakes. Barley was made into barley broth—a crucial staple in the Red River diet. Because export markets for grain did not exist, both field and garden crops "played somewhat similar roles," since the amount of each grown was still determined by family needs.[2] Foods growing in the wild supplemented farm produce. Saskatoons, chokecherries, pinchberries, strawberries, raspberries, blueberries, cranberries, wild apples, and plums were commonly used wild fruits. In March, some families made sugar from the sap of maples found in the loops of the Red and the Assiniboine rivers. Dried buffalo meat or pemmican was the main source of meat since most Red River settlers only occasionally slaughtered cattle. People also took occasional trips to Lake Manitoba to fish for whitefish.

Farm work is commonly described in terms of a seasonal round of activities involving the raising of crops. Descriptions have usually focussed on activities undertaken by men. The recollections of farm women who lived in the Red River Settlement[3] show the seasonal round of women's activities. As one of the Red River women noted, "We had our work for each season of the year, which kept us always busy."[4] June was a busy month as a garden had to be put in. Gardening not only involved seeding and harvesting, but weeding and watering as well. Weeding was particularly time-consuming. Men and women probably cooperated in gardening.[5] Next in the cycle of seasonal activities came haying, which usually took place in July and August. Hay cutting itself appears to have been done by the men, especially when it involved week-long stays off the farmstead. This usually occurred in late July or early August, when the men went out to cut extra hay on the open plains. "Before the day fixed for the beginning of hay cutting each year, the best hay meadows were spied out, and each man had planned where he was to cut hay.... The men went out and camped on the prairie in tents, riding home every Saturday evening for the Sunday."[6] Within the immediate vicinity of the farm, women joined in raking and stacking hay. One Red River woman recalled how the "girls used to go out with the boys to the hay meadows . . . and help in gathering up the hay. We had home-made rakes. We carried the hay to the stacks on poles, and after the stack was up we laid branches of trees over it so the wind would not blow the hay away before it settled down and became solid."[7] Another witnessed a farm couple making hay and recalled that the "wife was up on a high hay stack and he was pitching the hay up to her."[8] Historian Barry Kaye has noted that the "quantity of hay each settler could harvest was severly limited by the shortage of hired labour. A few Indians from St. Peter's sometimes hired themselves out at this busy time but haying was essentially a family affair in which both women and youngsters regularly took part."[9] In 1882, "only ten percent of the farmers at Red River, consisting of men of 'large means,' were able to hire labour for haymaking and harvesting. The rest had to rely wholly on family labour."[10]

Although the important role of women in haymaking is not always acknowledged in histories of the period, female participation in this work process was essential on the majority of farms. This becomes evident when the economic role of haying on Red River subsistence farms is considered. Haying was an important subsistence activity, especially in the early years of the Red River Settlement when grain crop productivity was very low. "Some animal feed was produced from the settlement's arable farming; in good crop years a little barley and oats were used as feed, potato surpluses were sometimes used to fatten pigs and sheep, and the straw of the threshed grain was occasionally fed to oxen. But the colonists were almost entirely dependent on the wild hay that they could bring in from the plains to feed their livestock in winter."[11] Kaye has shown the close correlation between livestock numbers and hay quantities available to farm families in the Red River Settlement.[12] The more hay you could harvest, the better your chances for livestock survival were and the more secure was your dairy, wool, and traction supply. Hay acted as the fuel that indirectly kept farm and family going. Therefore, the participation of all family members in haymaking should be valued equally.

Women were also important to haymaking in an indirect way. They carried on with farm and household chores while the men were out haying. As early as July, the men would travel to the open plains, called the "common," to start mowing. In dry years, they had to travel some sixty miles or more to get to suitable hay patches, making their stay off the farmsteads of long duration. After mowing, they "had to make numerous journeys hauling it by cart or sledge to the riverside farms.... [The] hauling of hay (and timber) was an almost daily activity of Red River livestock farmers during the winter."[13] With the men away, women had sole responsibility for the family and farm during part of the summer and most of the winter, carrying on many crucial subsistence activities other than haying. Women's and men's work, therefore, was interdependent. While the men were mowing, women, with the help of children, herded the cows and sheep, tended to the gardens, and performed a host of other daily tasks. In addition, they supplemented the food on the farm by gathering and preserving wild plants, herbs, and fruit. As one of the Red River women recalled: "We had to preserve our berries by drying. We used to dry raspberries, saskatoons and blueberries."[14] One woman described how the wild potato and the wild turnip were used in times of food shortage. Some country provisions were used for making medicine. The inner bark of the red willow was used in making a poultice for a swelling and the inner bark of the poplar was eaten as a tonic. In the early days of the Red River Settlement, an Aboriginal remedy made from the sap of the white spruce was used for scurvy.

In the fall came harvesting. Men, women, and children worked together once the wheat, barley, and oats were ready for reaping. Morton wrote that "[when] the reapers moved into the parks with their sickles and scythes . . . the women and children followed, raking, binding, and stooking...."[15] A French Canadian woman recalled that "[the] grain was cut with scythes and sickles. When the women helped, they used the sickles. We bound the sheaves with willow; we were careful not to lose, or waste, any of the precious grain."[16] Women's participation in harvesting was essential, given the technological and environmental conditions under which harvesting occurred and the biological tendency of wheat to shatter easily. Several women from the Kildonan site of the Red River Settlement recounted, for example, that

> in harvest time, the thing that made it necessary for those of the women
> who could do that work to assist was that the wheat we had then was an
> English white wheat with a larger berry than the wheat grown in the
> West today, which made good flour, but shelled very easily. A strong wind
> would leave a great many of the grains on the ground and in handling the
> sheaves in the carts a great deal of the wheat would fall out. On account
> of the danger of frost and also because of the slow method of harvesting,
> the cutting of the wheat when it was ready to be cut had to be done as
> soon as possible.[17]

It was a common sight to see women reaping grain, as the remarks of one of the first Grey Nuns to arrive in the Red River Settlement show. "In the next summer when it was harvest time . . . the sisters were out cutting the wheat by hand in our field next to the convent, working like the other women in the settlement who helped in the harvest. . . ."[18] For women, fieldwork was an extra chore, added to responsibilities at home and with livestock in the barnyard. The harvest season must have been especially busy. One Red River woman pointed out that when "we worked in the fields there was always a great deal to be done in the evening after the field work was over. The milk had to be attended to and the skim milk fed to the calves and the butter churned. . . . [Moreover, in] the fall, after the slaughtering, there was a great deal of work to be done in making blood puddings and white puddings and in boiling and drying tripe and getting our whole winter's supply of meat ready."[19] Women's work in harvesting garden crops and preserving the produce also coincided with harvest time in the grain fields.

In the late fall and during part of the winter, grain had to be threshed, winnowed, and, in the case of wheat, ground. "Threshing was done by flail on the barn floor; where one was lacking, on an ice floor; the grain was winnowed and sifted in the open air, and stored for grinding or for seed. . . . The wheat when threshed had still to be ground. In the early days hand mills had been used, and had to be kept as standbys, for times when roads were blocked, or wind or water [for the operation of the mills] failed."[20] The personal recollections of Red River women illustrate the gender roles in grain processing. With respect to threshing and winnowing, it was noted that "the men would go out to the barns to thresh with a flail. . . . Among the winter nights' occupations for the girls . . . was 'knocking barley.' The barley was put in the hollowed, bowl-like block of wood which was used for this purpose, and the girls would take turns, some in pounding it with a long-headed wooden mallet with a stick or a long-handled spoon. When the grain was all separated from the hulls it was winnowed, and was then ready for use in making barley broth."[21] In wheat grinding, the use of a hand mill made of two stones called a 'quern' was mentioned. "Jesus had it in mind when he said: 'Two women shall be grinding at the mill; the one shall be taken and the other left.' The women of Kildonan ground thus at the mill, in the time before there were windmills in the settlement; and the quern was often in use even after there were windmills."[22] After grinding came bolting (sifting). A Red River woman recalled that for "many years the windmills were the only mills. Sometimes there would be a breeze strong enough to give them power to grind, but not to bolt. . . . When we had to do the bolting ourselves we used to do it with a sieve of brass wire which we would hang from a beam and spread a white cloth under it on a table, then by pouring in the ground but unbolted grist we had brought from the mill and shaking the sieve we would get flour."[23]

In the winter, women were busy manufacturing cloth and clothing. This work process included taking care of the sheep that provided wool, the primary raw material. A Red River woman recalled that one of the chores done by girls every morning before school was feeding farm animals.[24] In summertime, when the sheep were out in the pasture, one of the evening chores was bringing the sheep home.[25] Women were also involved in sheep shearing in June. From the stories of Red River women it appears that the preparation of wool for clothmaking was done in the winter evenings.

One woman recalled that, when she was young, the girls had to tease wool after school in the afternoon. This wool was later carded by the women.[26] Spinning, knitting, weaving, and sewing came next. Most of the clothes and blankets were made out of homespun cloth. Mrs. Good, an eighty-three-year-old Red River woman, described the steps involved in making blankets. "We used to get sturgeon oil from the Indians in birch bark rogans and put it in the wool to make it work easier . . . and then when the blankets were made we had to wash the oil out of the wool. We used to have an enormous tub into which we put the blankets and soap and water and the girls would get in in their bare feet and tread on the blankets, and when that had been done long enough the girls would put on their stockings and shoes and then the boys would wring the blankets out."[27] The manufacture of clothing by women also included shoemaking. A Red River woman recalled that "Every article I wore was the product of my mother's hands, even my shoes, until I was fourteen or fifteen years old, when I got my first bought shoes."[28] Boots were made from tanned cattle hides. Buffalo or cattle sinew was used to stitch together the cut-out leather. Women tanned the leather themselves using willow bark and a tanning tub, which was usually an old, dug-out tree.

Women's care of clothing did not end with the manufacture of cloth and clothing. It also included maintenance, which was done through mending, laundering, and ironing.[29] Homespun materials were more durable, so women may have had to mend less often. However, garments were subjected to rough handling on the farmsteads and since Red River families were large, some having well over ten children, the pile of garments to be mended must still have been considerable. Red River women probably also laundered less often than their later counterparts. Cowan has suggested that "[prior] to industrialization, much of the clothing that people wore was virtually unwashable: the woven woolen goods, the alpacas and felts and leathers of which outer clothing was made, were cleaned by brushing; and the linen or knitted wools of which underclothing was composed, although potentially washable, were in fact rarely laundered."[30] Only very prosperous Red River farm families acquired part of their clothing materials from the Hudson's Bay Company store. A few families received packages of textiles from family overseas. These fabrics were often lighter and easier to wash and were, perhaps, more frequently laundered by women. Laundering was demanding. It involved the heavy tasks of fetching water from an outdoor source using pails and getting fuel for the wood stove in order to heat the water. It also involved several other tasks, as the recollections of Alberta pioneer Kathleen Strange of the early 1900s show:

Washing! What a job that always was. Usually it took me the entire day....The boiling, sudsy water had to be carried in pails from the stove to wherever my tubs were set. More than once I burned myself severely, spilling water on unprotected hands and legs....At the beginning I had washed by hand, rubbing laboriously on a board and earning for myself a frightful backache at the end of each dreaded washday.... Drying the clothes was almost as much of a job as washing them, especially in winter. It often took the best part of a week, and for many months during the year, when the weather was cold, the various rooms of our house were made uncomfortable and unpleasant with smelly underwear and clumsy flannel shirts which took not hours but days to air thoroughly.[31]

Without the use of bleach, laundering was especially cumbersome as "the whitest wash was achieved by setting the undies to simmer on the back burner."[32] Soap for laundering was not readily available and had to be made from scratch. Soapmaking was a work process in itself, which included the preparation of beef fat and ashes. It had to be performed with great care, as this description by McClung suggests:

The leach was a small barrel of ashes, set up on a trestle, high enough to cover a black iron pan. The barrel had small auger holes bored in the bottom, and the innumerable pails of water poured on the ashes would at last run through in reluctant black drops, and then the leach was said to be running. The lye thus extracted was used for making soap, and the day the soap was made was a day of high adventure. The operation took place outside in a big black kettle that was never used for anything else. No ordinary day would do; it had to be a clear bright day with no wind, and the moon had to be on the increase or the soap might not set. Over a blazing fire, made in a hole lined with stones, the grease and lye were fused in the old black pot and stirred all the time, from left to right, with a hickory stick. They used beef grease to make the soap soft....There was a fascination in the fiery boiling of this billowy mass, threatening every minute to boil over. My mother, in a sprigged blue print dress, tucked tightly between her knees and her head rolled in a red handkerchief stood on the windward side, stirring with a quick motion. Wooden boxes stood ready to receive the soap when it was done. No one must speak to her or interrupt in any way when the boiling was going on, for there was a moment when the pot must be removed and if that moment were correctly guessed the soap would harden. My mother was the High Priestess of all domestic rites to me, so of course she knew the exact moment.[33]

Starch for pressing clothing was made from scratch as well. As one Red River woman remarked, "we made our own starch from potatoes. We used to grind the potatoes and press them through a straining cloth stretched over a tub half filled with water, and let the starch settle. We put indigo in the starch for laundry use. We used to make starch for puddings separately."[34] Ironing was an additional aspect of the laundering work process. Several Red River women recalled the frills on their *mutches* (headwear), which they used to iron with a special iron called the "Italian" iron.[35] Having no electricity, they used the stove as a heat source. Ironing, therefore, involved the additional task of maintaining a hot wood stove.

Many of women's tasks were carried out throughout the year. Mending, laundering, and ironing were done at regular intervals. So was candlemaking, which involved the preparation of tallow on a hot stove. Housecleaning was a daily responsibility, carried out with thoroughness on a weekly basis. Baking, too, was done at least once a week. Child care, on the other hand, was a twenty-four-hour responsibility. Children had to be dressed, bathed, fed, and brought up in the ways of the community. Since families were big, there was a lot of work involved. Without disposable baby bottles and diapers, prepared baby foods, running water, or washing machines, baby care was particularly labour-intensive, as this quote illustrates: "Mothers would naturally breastfeed their babies, if they could. If they were unable to produce enough milk, they would have to substitute animal milk, since wet nurses were not common. In the days before disposable baby bottles, animal horns and bottles with wash leather nipples were used. Rubber nipples did not appear until mid century."[36] Once the baby began to eat solid food there was the additional job of preparing special baby food. This involved long hours of boiling grain or oatmeal, followed by drying, sifting, and boiling again. In addition, baby's napkins and diapers, as well as those of two- or three-year-old toddlers, added volume to the pile of garments to be laundered.

Preparing meals and cleaning up after them were other daily routines. So were milking and livestock care, as this description by a Red River woman shows. "The girls had chores to do every evening and every morning, too, before school. We all used to get up very early ... and the girls would help in milking the cows and feeding them, and in feeding the calves and pigs."[37] Another woman noted some of the different tasks involved in the milking. "We were up at five ... and attended to the milk which had been left standing overnight in the milk coolers. They were wooden pans made of oak each with two handles. Every morning we washed them first with cold water, and then with warm water, using a strong home-made willow brush, and last with boiling water. Then we set them to air, ready for the evening. We used to have two sets of coolers."[38] Considering that water had to be fetched from an outside source and the stove heated up for the second and third rinsing, the cleaning of wooden milk coolers was not easy. It is not surprising that the introduction of tin pans was welcomed. A Red River woman remarked, "It was not until the Company began to make tin pans at York Factory that our work was made very much easier for us by the use of tin pans, which were so much easier to clean instead of the old oak coolers."[39] Milk was used for drinking and making butter and cheese. Butter- and cheesemaking were weekly chores. Buttermaking was a time-consuming and laborious work process. It involved several different, yet interrelated, tasks. This is illustrated by the following description:

> For buttermaking you used sour cream and churned it until it curdled. The children did it [churning] once a week. It takes about one hour but the time depends on the cream and how warm it is. The churn was a broomstick with cross-piece boards that were worked up and down in the churn. Buttermaking takes time, depending on many things like the temperature of the cream, the sourness of the cream, whether there is still some milk in the cream, like if it was creamed off badly, and the size of the churn. Also, the thicker the cream, the faster it would go. Old country cream had higher butter fat. [After you have churned the cream into butter] you work the butter. You drain the buttermilk out. You wash it [the butter], so you put very cold water in the butter and you had to work it and it [the butter] got very solid. You drained that water again. Then, you had to work that butter to get all the water out because water will spoil the butter. We always used wooden bowls and butter-ladles for that. The butter was at one end of the tub and you pressed the water out and the butter [simultaneously] to the other end [of the tub]. Then, you threw out the water. That was repeated five or six times; as long as you saw bubbles of water in the butter. That would take half an hour or three quarters of an hour, depending on the amount of butter you had to do. You sprinkled in some salt and reworked it [the butter] after the salt had had a chance to dissolve.[40]

Like buttermaking, cheesemaking required skill and specialized knowledge. Red River women recalled making cheese "on Saturday, using the rennet which we prepared from the stomachs of calves."[41] They probably also made cottage cheese. Helen, one of several contemporary farm women who made cottage cheese in the past, remarked that the production of cottage cheese "needs patience and timing—when it is heated too much it will curdle and get hard." She also said that cheesemaking "took a lot of time." The work process involved in making cottage cheese was described by Olga. "We made cheese out of milk. You put it to sour and then put it on the stove and heat it up. What we used to do with cottage cheese; we put the cheese in a bag, let it drip off and then work at it and then add cream. That made it very delicious. Then we used to pack it in wooden pails. We made a few pails for the winter." Milk, butter, and cheese, provided largely by women, were crucial dietary supplements in Red River households. With the exception of butter, they were protein-rich foods and supplied high-quality animal protein without any precious livestock having to be killed. Moreover, women bartered dairy products at the Hudson's Bay Company store for household necessities and farm supplies. Just how important dairy products were to Red River settlers is demonstrated by the fact that, upon marriage, a cow or heifer was usually given to the bride.

Apart from their work on the farmstead, Red River women played a major role in community life as well. At weddings, dances, fairs, and other social events women were generally responsible for the provision of food. They helped each other out in times of illness and childbirth. Several women were also quite active in educational, church, and charitable activities. Some were teachers, some were in the church choir, and some were active in the St. Boniface orphanage and hospital.

Women's work was crucial to daily existence and general social well-being in the Red River Settlement. Subsistence farming called forth a division of labour in which men and women had complementary responsibilities and in which a high degree of task sharing took place. Together, they made survival in isolation on the prairies possible by providing their own necessities such as food, shelter, and clothing.

Women's Work on Pioneer Farms

In 1870, Manitoba became the first prairie province of Canada but, as historian Gerald Friesen has pointed out, the destiny of the prairies had been determined long before:

> The millions of acres of western real estate were expected to serve the interests of "old Canada," in the view of those who lived east of Lake Superior. . . . Because previous economic booms had accompanied the expansion of agricultural settlement, they planned to establish a new 'investment frontier' that would open the west and enrich the east in one fell swoop. Their hopes lay with the pioneer farmer who, far from being the self-sufficient recluse of folk-tales, would initiate an economic take-off by buying lumber, groceries, and agricultural implements, on the one hand, and shipping grain and livestock, on the other.[42]

The federal government of Sir John A. Macdonald devised a National Policy to ensure this profitable development of the West. Federal policy on settlement affected agricultural development and therefore gender roles in prairie farming. In an effort to encourage settlement, the homestead system was adopted in 1872 under the Dominion Lands Act. Settlers received a 160-acre homestead for ten dollars. By 'proving up' the homestead within three years, they could clear the title and own the land. Government regulations stated that, to 'prove up' the homestead, thirty acres of land had to be broken and a house worth three hundred dollars or more had to be built within three years. Historians have generally overlooked the fact that women could not qualify for a homestead in their own name. Yet, "[unlike] the United States, Canada did not open homesteads to wives or single women. Only if she were the head of a household could a woman, like any male over eighteen, earn title to a quarter section of land by farming it. A wife or daughter might toil alongside her menfolk, contributing equally to the fulfillment of the homestead requirements, but in the end, the men owned the land."[43] Women were legally defined as dependents. They owned no property, and had no income according to the legal system. Their livelihood was therefore necessarily embedded within wifehood. Wifehood usually meant motherhood and thus population growth. This is what the Dominion government wanted to achieve. As one immigration commissioner put it, "It is not independent women we want but rather population."[44]

The first few years on a homestead meant hard work. Especially prior to 1881, when the railway was built, pioneer families had to make a living with very little outside help, just as Red River Settlement families did before them. Towns and country stores did not yet exist. Because domestic markets were absent and export markets inaccessible, people were forced to be self-sufficient through mixed farming. Other factors kept prairie farming within subsistence limits as well. The early pioneers were not familiar with the environmental conditions they faced. The heavy clay and tough sod of the Red River Valley proved to be too much for their ploughs and they struggled with a short growing season. Their manual farm technology resembled that of farm families in the Red River Settlement. Traction power for plough and cart was provided by slow-moving oxen. Haying continued to be done by scything and hand raking, although mechanical mowers and rakes were soon introduced. Few mechanical reapers were used in grain harvesting, so the scythe and cradle remained commonplace. Grain sheaves were still bound and stooked by hand and then hauled by cart to the barn. Some established farm families had a threshing machine that ran on horsepower but among newcomers the flail was used and winnowing done when the wind was right.

Subsistence farming on the frontier called forth a gender division of labour similar to that of farm families in the Red River Settlement. The daily, weekly, and seasonal activities of pioneer farm women resembled those of their earlier counterparts. However, an additional factor in farming on the frontier was the extra challenge of establishing a farm and community. Under conditions of extreme social and economic isolation and with only three years to prove up the homestead, pioneer women were heavily involved in breaking land for cultivation and constructing homes, barns, fences, and wells—all traditionally male responsibilities. In some cases, men arrived earlier than women and children and had already made a start on the work at hand. But often all members of a family arrived together. Since settlements were too sparse for neighbouring men to organize land-breaking and construction bees, and because hired help was not yet available and young families lacked able-bodied sons, task sharing between men and women was imperative for success on the homestead.

Immediately upon arrival, settlers cleared and broke land for a vegetable garden in order to secure a supply of food. Ruth, whose family homesteaded in the Riding Mountain foothills, recalled that when her parents came to Canada, "the first thing they did was breaking and planting a garden together. They broke it together, but after that mother did all the garden work. We lived on potatoes and vegetables and faith in God." Annie, whose parents pioneered near Rathwell, recalled likewise that they "grew everything—peas, beets, potatoes, cabbage, corn, turnips, tomatoes, carrots and onions. If we wouldn't have grown our garden, we wouldn't have eat [sic]. Definitely not!" The degree of difficulty in breaking land depended on the area in which one settled. Thickly wooded soils were harder to break than prairie sod, demanding more participation by women. Helen, whose parents settled on the wooded slopes of Riding Mountain, noted that "there was nothing but bush. All we saw was the sky. Men and women, they all worked together. Clearing the land was done with horses and oxen. They [horses and oxen] were on a stump and pulled and pulled. And the women used to pick up the wood and throw it on piles. Coming home, mother used to be black from burning wood." Ruth, who babysat her siblings while her parents were clearing land with a pick for digging out roots, recalled that "at night mother came home with blood running down her hands." Another pioneer woman recounted that the "women worked just as hard as the men. The men would dig around the trees and then the women would pull them out with a rope around their waist and the tree."[45]

The autobiography of Alberta pioneer woman Peggy Holmes describes how she and her husband Harry established a farm under frontier conditions.

On their construction activities, Holmes wrote: "We drew up yards of plans for the log house, barns, chickenhouse, pig pens, well site, vegetable garden, flower garden, fences. . . . [We] decided to begin digging our own well on the spot where I had predicted water would be found. With bucket and shovel, rope and pulley, plus our two pairs of hands, the first feet down were not too difficult . . . I as foreman-helper was instructed to haul up the full buckets of clay, empty them and return them."[46] She continued:

> While Harry was building pole corrals and shelter for stock, I was peeling logs. . . . With a two-handled drawknife you sit astride a log and peel off its bark. You have to keep rolling the logs. Harry [sawed the logs] with a one-man cross-cut saw, chopping the corners with an axe. . . . [Constructing the walls of our home necessitated the use of ropes which had to] go under a log and over the wall, with me on the other side of the building driving Skin and Grief [two horses] which were hooked on to the ropes. Harry would yell to me, "Git up" and, "Whoa," and guide the log into its place. . . . [We] laid the floor as quickly as possible, much to the detriment of our knees. Housemaid's knee is painful, and we both had it! . . . We whipped up temporary shelters for chickens, and a log barn which was a gift from another desperate character on his way out. These logs were numbered and hauled over. . . . The next task was the chinking, which posed another problem as the ground was frozen . . . so with hod and trowel I stole into the barn and waited for material [cow dung] to be delivered, then dashed back into the house and whipped up a dollop. Everyday I collected my material and worked on the four walls.[47]

Peggy Holmes was also involved in digging a cellar under the house and thatching the roof. Her autobiography illustrates the pressures created by government regulations on proving up the homestead, which necessitated task sharing by men and women in making improvements. Towards the end of the three-year prove-up period, "Harry was on the last pull of the line fence, another half mile to go on our south boundary. We had to get this finished or the land would not be ours. . . . I went out to help Harry complete the fencing and [worked] feverishly against time. . . . We had just finished—and had proved up at last."[48]

Isolation and hard work with simple, often self-invented means characterized all areas of prairie settlement. In Manitoba's Interlake area, for example, Ukrainian pioneers built shelters with very few, simple tools. For lack of draught animals, women helped drag logs from the bush to the designated building site. Ukrainian historian Michael Ewanchuk noted that pioneer families "knew how to get along with little. A man and his wife could go into the bush with an axe and a spade and little more and make a home for themselves."[49] After chinking the spaces between the logs with moss, "the walls of the house were plastered, outside and in."[50] Plastering walls was generally a woman's job. They would make a mud plaster using clay, sand, grass, and water. Betty, a Ukrainian farm woman who was well over ninety years of age at the time of the interview and was still living in the original log house on her Interlake homestead, related how she and her husband had built and plastered their home together. Olga, whose parents pioneered on the southern slopes of Riding Mountain, had plastered several houses in her lifetime. In addition to plastering, "the women cut reeds with sickles and bound them into sheaves which were used to thatch the roof."[51] In the non-wooded areas of Manitoba, sod became the main building block. Some of the first Mennonite houses in southern Manitoba in the 1870s were built of sod. A Saskatchewan example perhaps typifies women's involvement in the construction of farm buildings using sod:

> The children and I built our first sod barn. It was only 14 x 14 feet but it was necessary to have a place to put the cow. The job was hard and we did not have hardly anything to work with. We had gotten a fire guard broken and it was from this that we got the necessary sod. The two oldest children carried the sod between them on a board and I did the building. As this was an exceedingly slow way, as the poor children could not carry enough to keep me busy, I made a harness for the cow and made her help us in hauling the sod. This was a little better but as the harness was not very substantial, it was breaking continually and made things very trying. I had a job every evening of either repairing the old harness or making a new one. The utensils I had to make the sod level with consisted of an old butcher knife and the sticks which were lying around. Finally it was completed and a roof was made from poplar poles which we managed to get out of the valley nearby.[52]

Frontier conditions demanded a high labour input from women. Carolyn E. Sachs, who did an historical study of American farm women, remarked: "On the frontier, women were expected to work with their husbands until the homestead was established."[53] This description applies very well to Canadian frontier women. In fact, the type of work performed by women on the frontier suggests that "there is a loosening of sex-role expectations. The requirements for survival necessitated the learning of new skills and the putting aside, or holding in abeyance, the traditional concepts of feminine behavior."[54] The author of this excerpt, anthropologist Seena B. Kohl, who studied farm women and their families in southwestern Saskatchewan, asserted, however, that "the loosening of sex-role definitions did not release women from their primary tasks: the maintenance of the household and the care of children."[55] Hence, women cleared, dug, and built, in addition to their numerous ongoing domestic responsibilities. Even child-bearing did not stop the flow of chores that had to be done. During the interview with Helen, she remarked that "women, they were pregnant and they were helping to clear land—they just had to get home in time to have a baby." Likewise, Ruth recalled how her mother, who was heavy with child, loaded cordwood onto a cart and took it into town by oxen. During childbirth, she said, the older children in the family carried on the chores for a while but "mother did not get much rest after childbirth." She remembered another incident when a neighbouring woman went out into the bush to get the cows and came home with a son in her apron. Having children and still doing chores was not easy on pioneer women. Ruth remarked that her mother had to help clear land in the bush but "with kids every year that was hard. My mother, one day while working in the garden, sat down and cried: 'My God, why did I ever come here to this mosquito land.'" The fact that pioneer women could not take any time off for child-bearing shows the high value placed on their labour. With husbands and children already doing their share of the work on the farm, women had little choice but to resume their activities as quickly as possible after giving birth.

Women's particular skills in carrying out essential subsistence work like dairying, gardening, preserving, cooking, making clothes, soap, candles, medicine, and so on, were indispensible. Towns where these specialized foods and services could be purchased were absent and other family members did not possess full knowledge of how to successfully carry out this work from start to finish. For example, a lot of skill and knowledge was required for making and administering medicines. Henry, a retired farm operator, remarked, "There were no doctors around, but my mother had ways. She picked up flowers, herbs and so on for the winter, to get over colds or to kill a fever. She made her own medicine. I still use a lot of those. We had a special flower on the farm that brought down fever." For common colds and minor injuries women used wild and cultivated plants for making salves and medicinal beverages. For example, a conconction of figs, coriander, and molasses was used against constipation. Dills and cucumber, but especially "pickled juice" were good for a cold, Mary said during an interview. Goosegrease was used as a chest salve to be rubbed on for a chest cold. Nellie McClung described one of her mother's remedies against an earache. "After the ear had been washed with soap and water, a few drops of laudanum were put in, and an onion was put in the ashes to roast, and when it was well heated through, it was cautiously put on the sore ear and bandaged with a white rag."[56] Women were knowledgeable about livestock health as well. They often used the same healing methods and potions for their cattle as for nursing their children and husbands. Doctors and veterinarians were not available. Hence, women developed veterinary skills as an extension of their traditional responsibility for child care and family well-being. This is illustrated by a comment by Mae Olstad, an Alberta pioneer. "You know I was the veterinary on the farm and every-thing else. . . . He was no good at that at all and so if any animal got sick it was me."[57] Similarly, Helen from Mountain Road told me, "I was a doctor for animals. Like when a sow got pigs, I watched them. We had eight sows. I also helped with calving."

Families deprived of adult women due to illness and death were seri-ously handicapped. Even though children and husbands assisted with cer-tain tasks such as chopping vegetables, milking, churning butter, or weeding the garden, women were the ones who knew how to orchestrate all the interrelated tasks of which their overall responsibilities were comprised. They knew how to preserve the vegetables, make butter and cheese out of milk, make soap out of ash and lard, or candles out of tallow. Without this knowledge and these skills, the provision of items to meet family needs was at jeopardy. Mary's family history illustrates this. In 1936 her mother died, leaving Mary, who was then twelve years old, in charge of ten younger children and the household. Although Mary had often assisted her mother with making soap, candles, and clothes, she was not qualified to carry out these responsibilities independently. When her mother passed away, these trades were lost to the family, making it less self-reliant and more depend-ent on commercial services. Fortunately, Mary's father could salvage home baking, having learned this from his mother. On the frontier it was practi-cally impossible to compensate for the loss of one's mother's or wife's skills with commercial goods and services. Yet, frontier conditions took a high toll on women. Women often bore a child every year while continuing to do heavy physical work. They had little opportunity to recuperate after childbirth and had little or no professional medical care. Women's mortality rate was high, so remarriage was frequent. One pioneer woman related, "Most men had two wives, as one woman usually wore out before the man did."[58] The marriage of widowers and widows was the most common type of remarrige and served a mutual, rather than a romantic, interest. Peggy Holmes's autobiography provides the example of "Herman Brueker, a lonely widower whose wife had died in childbirth leaving him with four young children. . . . Herman asked us to advertise for a wife for him. . . . 'I want you folks to help me get a new missus,' he announced. 'It ain't no use; I can't do everything on me own, what with the kids and the chores, and feeding the stock. I've got to get me a woman.'"[59]

Remarriage could be beneficial for both widower and widow, especially when they were left with young children. Frequent remarriage is strong evidence of the essential nature of the cooperation between farm women and their husbands and, particularly, of the specialized fund of knowledge held by farm women. Given the complementary division of knowledge and labour between men and women and, therefore, their mutual dependence, each regained the economic partner they had lost. Together they had all the knowledge and skills to make life on the frontier possible.

2.
The Passing of the Pioneer Period

The Transition to Commercial Agriculture

As more settlers moved into Manitoba, settlements became denser and less dispersed, reducing social isolation on the frontier. Railroad construction quickened the pace of settlement. Towns grew and became local markets for farm products. Railways also made foreign markets accessible, which, at the time, were seen as being virtually unlimited. Western Europe, and England in particular, became the largest export market for the hard spring wheat grown on the Canadian prairies, preferred for its excellent baking characteristics. Changes in wheat type and field technology enabled settlers to realize the commercial potential of wheat production. The new wheat variety had a shorter maturation period, making it less prone to early fall frosts, and yielded more per acre. The new, horse-drawn implements saved time. Gradually, the old-fashioned broadcasting method for sowing the fields gave way to seed drills. Reapers replaced scythes and sickles in the 1880s and these were, in turn, replaced by binders in the 1890s. Binders, requiring four to six horses for their draught, incorporated an automatic binding device that tied cut grain into sheaves, thus speeding up the harvesting process considerably. Horse-drawn sulky and gang ploughs replaced the walking-ploughs of earlier times. "The gang plough with its two furrows had become the standard plough for fields now mellow with five to ten or more years of tillage [by the 1890s]; the sulky was used for sod-breaking, while the walking-plough, the symbol of . . . of agriculture, was relegated to the hard tasks of brush breaking or the simple job of ploughing the garden and the potato patch."[1] With larger grain crops, the threshing outfit replaced the flail.

The adoption of new technology was not uniform across Manitoba. Pioneers settling at different times and in different parts of the province faced radically different conditions for farm development, affecting the rate at which the transition to commercial agriculture took place:

> [The] duration of the pioneer era in any district, and the rapidity with which settlements were established, were influenced by the initial productive capacity, the natural fertility, and the ease of workability of the various soils in the specific landscape areas under settlement. Where prairie soils were favorable for the production of products that could be marketed, many early pioneers . . . soon climbed to personal independence and financial success. In such cases prosperous agricultural districts were established fairly rapidly, and in such districts the pioneer era under which the first settlers lived was comparatively of short duration. Under these conditions many holdings soon became well established farms. . . . In other districts the local soil and natural features did not permit rapid land use development . . . the natural limitations of soil and other natural features inhibited, retarded, or favored only partial conversion of virgin soil areas to productive lands. In these districts pioneer conditions persisted for longer periods of time, so that successive operators with restricted opportunities and limited resources . . . were unable to acquire the affluence of those . . . [in] districts where a surplus over a livelihood from the "good earth" had been easier to obtain.[2]

The first wave of immigrants, nearly all of whom were well-to-do farm families from Ontario, arrived in the 1870s and 1880s and settled on the grasslands and parklands of south-central and southwestern Manitoba. These were some of the most fertile lands in the province and could be converted relatively easily into farmland. The upland plains, for example, were described as "prairie land which held neither stone nor stump to check the plough" and "deep soil to be had cheaply."[3]

Settlement was rapid on these prime farmlands. By the end of the 1880s, the British-Ontario way of life had become well established in southern Manitoba. "The boom [of the late 1870s and early 1880s] ended the pioneer days in southern agricultural Manitoba, and confirmed the work of the first decade. It left a community established with all its essential characteristics delineated; an agricultural province; in the majority populated with a British-Ontario stock. . . ."[4]

The deep and fertile soils of Dauphin Lake and surroundings extended the frontier of the first-wave settlers when the railway reached this area in 1896. Shortly thereafter, the fertile valley of the Swan River, between the Duck and Porcupine mountains, was settled. Here, too, agriculture quickly flourished as many "of the first comers were Manitobans moving out to their second frontier to pit the skills and capital of the first against the familiar hazards."[5] Anglo-Saxon settlers generally brought their own implements or purchased the necessary farm tools and livestock in Winnipeg before moving on to their new farmsteads. Local histories document the sometimes considerable amounts of money and possessions that were brought along from the East. For example, Mrs. Proven related: "I remember coming to Minnedosa in September of 1880, being eleven days driving from Winnipeg in a covered wagon. Father, mother, eight of us and a hired man, one team of horses, one team of oxen, one pony, in a Red River cart, and 65 head of cattle and oxen."[6] Nellie McClung's parents sold their farm of "one-hundred-and-fifty stony acres" in Grey County, Ontario, to settle on 800 acres of parkland at the Souris mouth, in Manitoba.[7] They arrived with two wagonloads of "settler's effects," which included "anything from a plow to a paper of pins" and, after buying oxen, wagons, and supplies in Winnipeg, they still had $1600 left.[8] This was a solid base from which to develop the new farmstead. Within three years, Nellie McClung's parents invested in a binder to replace an old, second-hand reaper and had one team of horses in addition to the oxen. With the new machine and faster moving horses working productive farmland, their farm could expand quickly. This appears to have been common in the area as a whole because the author noted that her father and several neighbours purchased six binders simultaneously, collecting them in Brandon on the same day.[9]

Anglo-Saxons were joined by other, less populous, ethnic groups among the first wave of settlers. French Canadians, Scandinavians, Icelanders, Germans, Belgians, and other continental Europeans also arrived. Among them, Mennonite settlers formed a particularly distinct group. In 1874, thousands arrived in southern Manitoba and settled on two reserves, one on the west side of the Red River and the other on the east side. Again, the combination of settling on good farmland and possessing some starting capital proved to be successful. "These simple and sturdy folk, not without suffering and heavy labour, were soon masters of their new-old environment and prosperous in self-sufficient plenty. Like the bulk of the Ontario settlers, they had been well-to-do farmers in their homeland, and had a modest amount of capital."[10] It is noted in the local history of Blumenfeld that, upon arrival in Manitoba, "the first sixty-five families spent $20,000 in three days, the most costly items being wagons and horses."[11] The average family in the East Reserve was well-off and, although the settlers in the West Reserve were generally poor, a substantial loan of $26,000 from Ontario Mennonites improved their overall financial position considerably. In addition, the Canadian government provided Mennonite settlers with a sum of $260,000 towards travelling and immigration expenses, and gave them an additional loan of $100,000 to pay for food, implements, and supplies. "The two loans, referred to as the 'Brotschuld' (debt for bread), made it possible for the Mennonite settlements to survive and to accelerate in economic growth and independence"[12] As soon as the opportunity arose, Mennonite farm families mechanized their farms. In 1878, reapers already replaced scythes for cutting grain, soon followed by binders. The first horse- and steam-powered threshing outfits replaced the flails in 1877 and oxen were making room for horses. By 1882, only one Blumenfeld farm family still owned two oxen.[13] No doubt, the combination of settling on prime farmland and possessing some material resources enabled many first-wave settlers to ex-pand and mechanize their farms at an early date. They benefitted from the economic boom of the late 1870s and first half of the 1880s, and invested their growing income in more equipment and draught animals.

The quality of farmland, the starting capital, and the proximity to rail-ways and other roads enjoyed by first-wave farmsteaders stands in sharp contrast to conditions faced by pioneers who came around the turn of the century. Among them, Ukrainian immigrants were the most numerous. "Their separateness was intensified by the fact that the remaining home-stead and cheap lands of Manitoba lay along the bushland frontier extend-ing from the southeastern corner of the province to Lake Winnipeg, up through Interlake district, and northwestward around Lake Manitoba to the slopes of Riding and Duck Mountains. Into these rugged bushlands the new settlers went of necessity...."[14]

The wooded land of the Interlake region was difficult to clear, thereby lengthening the time necessary for establishing a farm. Some of it was unsuitable for wheat production, and the lack of roads and railways hin-dered development. In addition, isolation from trading centres and grain elevators made access to supplies and markets more difficult. Likewise, the southern slopes of Riding Mountain, labelled a "chronic fringe area," were "so handicapped by broken topography, inferior soils, and unfavorable cli-mate that it [remained] a sparsely populated and marginal type of settle-ment after half a century of pioneering."[15] The unfavourable conditions for farming in the remaining settlement areas discouraged the rapid develop-ment of commercial grain operations. Moreover, many Ukrainian pioneers "left behind a world of poverty and carried with them little material wealth."[16] They had few resources to invest in farm development and lacked the financial support offered to first-wave settlers. It "took many years be-fore they could attain the financial status of the farmers living on better lands. This situation was not due to the poorer lands alone. It was also due to the fact that they did not receive any governmental transportation and other assistance on the par with the settlers of other groups. This placed them in less favorable positions to that of the Mennonites. . . ."[17] Not surprisingly, many East-European immigrants were unable to quickly reach the prosperity levels of their southern neighbours. Their farms remained smaller in size and less mechanized than those of the earlier settlers. Walking-ploughs, scythes, and sickles were standard field implements for most East-European settlers, who could not yet afford the sophisticated equipment, such as binders and gang ploughs, used on southern farms. Many continued to use the broadcasting method for seeding the fields and the flail for threshing the crop. As a result, pioneer life lingered on for these settlers, perpetuating a division of labour based on subsistence farming, in which men and women continued to work side by side in the fields and barnyards. This was no longer the case among the more properous first-wave settlers, however.

Women's Work on Early Commercial Farms

On the prime agricultural lands of the province, an increasing focus on commercial grain production changed the roles of men and women in farming by altering the scope of various farm labour processes. Women's direct participation in field-crop production declined due to "push" and "pull" factors. Push factors are those that displaced women from fieldwork. Pull factors, on the other hand, are those that drew women away from fieldwork by placing greater demands on their time in the home and barnyard.

A major factor pushing women out of fieldwork was the growing presence of male workers in the field. As families mechanized their farms and expanded their grain acreage, they needed more labour, especially at harvest time. Steam-powered threshing machines required many people with special skills for their operation. An engineer, tank-man, and fireman were needed to supervise the power supply from the steam tractor to the belt-driven thresher. Bandcutters, pitchers, and a feeder helped supply the wheat to the threshing machine, while others led teams of horses that hauled the wheat to the outfit and the separated grain to the bins. A bagger-man put the grain in bags, and another person, a strawbucker, hauled away the straw. All in all, there could be well over twenty people involved in one threshing operation. Even though neighbours helped each other at harvest time, there was a general labour shortage in rural communities. To reduce this problem, the immigration branch of the Manitoba Department of Agriculture and the railway companies cooperated after 1890 to bring thousands of men from eastern Canada on special harverst-excursion trains each year. In addition, a steady labour supply became available from the newly opened frontier areas in Manitoba throughout the growing season. East-European immigrants from the Interlake region, for example, offered their labour on southern farms. "Farms in the prairie area needed men to help with seeding and harvesting. Every spring saw an exodus of men from the Gimli area to work on the extra-gang crews or as section hands. Some went to work for large farmers for a period of eight months.... At first the Ukrainian farmers depended on the Mennonites for their employment, but when the Anglo-Saxon farmers learned about their skills as harvesters they went farther west where they were paid better wages.... Each summer many ... left for southwestern Manitoba to work on the harvest fields."[18] Likewise, Ukrainian settlers on southern slopes of Riding Mountain and to the northwest of Strathclair worked as threshers in the south. Gradually, these labourers and those from the East displaced women from fieldwork on prosperous farms. Here, grain production grew into an exclusively male endeavour, a trend that started before the turn of the century and continued on in the twentieth century. In fact, on early Mennonite farms, women's participation in fieldwork seems to have been minimal from the start. These first-wave pioneers settled in Manitoba in large groups—sometimes comprising whole villages from their native country—and quickly established their traditional communities on the frontier by adapting their Russian agricultural pattern of village-controlled and communally cultivated farmland to the Canadian situation.[19] This village-based settlement system facilitated the formation of male work 'bees' to break land, build lodgings, raise barns and so on. The experience of first-wave Mennonite pioneer women is likely to have been different from that of Anglo-Saxon women who pioneered under conditions of isolation on remote homesteads. It was probably also different from that of a later wave of Mennonite pioneer women who arrived in Manitoba during the 1920s. The village-agricultural system of communally cultivated farmland had virtually disintegrated by that time. Many, if not all, male work 'bees' had been dismantled, and farm families were on their own to work the land, unless they could afford to employ workers. Having settled in Manitoba with few assets and without the benefit of the loans their predecessors had enjoyed, these poorer, second-wave Mennonite families had to rely on women's labour in the fields. The more prosperous Mennonite farm families and their Anglo-Saxon counterparts of the 1870s, however, employed male labourers to help with the expanding fieldwork, thus displacing women's labour. In addition, after ten to twenty years of settlement, many first-generation pioneer families now had grown-up sons who began to take over their mothers' shares in fieldwork. On Nellie McClung's family farm, her father and two oldest brothers initially did all the fieldwork during the growing season. At that time, they had only eighty acres of land under cultivation. But when this acreage was expanded, they hired help instead of enlisting the women in the family, since a total of nine men had arrived in the farming district to work as farm labourers.[20]

Interviews with farm women also illustrate the dominance of males in fieldwork. Jodie of Niverville told me that neither she nor her mother nor grandmother had ever performed any fieldwork. On the farm of her grandparents, who came to Manitoba in the 1880s and settled south of Winnipeg, fieldwork was carried out by males only. On Jodie's parental farm, too, fieldwork was done by her father and three brothers during the growing season and with the help of male neighbours at threshing time. Maureen of the Miami area also related that, during the early 1900s when she was a child, her mother and the neighbouring farm women never worked in the grain fields. She said, "In our area I don't remember any women doing fieldwork. Mother never worked outside." She added that, because the farms in her area were generally well off, women did not have to do any "outside" work. On her parental farm there was always a hired man to assist her father and brothers with the fieldwork in spring and summer. In the fall, "the threshing gang would come in from the East by train," and again, only males were involved in this field task. Similarly, Nicole, whose parents farmed near Russell, related: "I didn't grow up to do the manual labour [in the field] on the farm because I had three brothers." She added that after her marriage, when she and her husband settled on a farm near Minnedosa, she continued to have little to do with fieldwork because her husband and his two brothers did that work. In later years her two sons assisted in the fields.

Similar comments about the relationship between farm prosperity, the ability to hire help, and women's reduced fieldwork participation were made by other farm women during interviews with them. There was a general consensus that women's direct involvement in field tasks depended on the availability and affordability of male help. It was only during periods of war and economic depression that some of these women became involved in fieldwork. Several mentioned helping with stooking and harrowing during times of male-labour shortage. Sandy of Rathwell remarked, for example, "You had no money. Everybody was in the same situation. During the 1930s mom and dad had it hard. The family did everything. There was no such thing as hired help. Dad was the main one to work out in the field. Mother never worked with the threshing machine in the field but she stooked out in the field. We all did." Some women commented, however, that, despite the economic depression in the 1930s, "there was lots of help on the farm." Unemployed "citymen" worked in the fields for twenty dollars a month, an amount that was partly subsidized by the provincial government. So, even in the 1930s, those farm families who could afford to hire help could keep their women out of the grain fields.

Farm prosperity appears to have been a factor in the gradual displacement of women from field tasks in the United States as well. A study by Carolyn Sachs of the historical and present-day role of women in American agriculture has indicated that similar forces were at work. The increasing focus on commercial production in farming, accompanied by farm expansion and mechanization, made the employment of field aids who were males both financially possible and necessary. Based on various agricultural reports and numerous rural studies covering the nineteenth century and early twentieth century, the author concluded that "when extra help could be hired, women left the fields for the home."[21] Moreover, she argued that "middle-class" and "well-to-do" farm women rarely engaged in fieldwork.[22] This coincides with my own research findings for Manitoba. The more prosperous farm families in the south of Manitoba not only received help at threshing time but could afford to hire labour throughout the growing season. Manitoba historian Gerald Friesen affirmed that Manitoba's rural society, at the turn of the century, was characterized by a social hierarchy of wealth and status. "In the top level of this hierarchy were families …[that] possessed large farms and considerable material wealth; they were sustained by the labour of a number of male and female 'hired hands.' The next level of the hierarchy was occupied by the respectable families whose farms approximated the district average in size and who might employ one or two labourers during the growing season."[23] These upper two strata were to be found on the most productive farmland of Manitoba.

Probably the most noticeable factor that pulled women away from fieldwork on expanding farms was a dramatic increase in subsistence production and domestic work related to the growth in the workforce on the farm. Farm women usually cooked, laundered, and cleaned for hired men who had board and room on the farm during the growing season. They also cooked for the threshers in the fall who, depending on the size of the crop and the weather, would stay on the farm anywhere from several days to several weeks. A great deal of planning and labour took place long before the threshing crew arrived on the farm. Farm women had to calculate how much extra food was needed beyond family needs to feed the work crew. For example, Olga, who fed the threshers on chicken meat, related that "with all the workers and the kids you would be surprised. Two roosters and two chickens was not hardly enough a day. During threshing time we had thirteen or fourteen men for a few days and I needed a lot of chickens to feed them. In total, we used about two hundred chickens a year." It is clear that the tasks involved in raising poultry increased in volume in response to the growing food needs on the farm. With more chickens to be raised for consumption, there was more work involved in watching the hens' behaviour to determine when they are ready to hatch eggs, in collecting the eggs for redistribution to the 'clockers,' in feeding the chickens, in cleaning the chicken coop, in monitoring the new chicks, in slaughtering, plucking, dressing, and, finally, in preserving the meat by cutting it in small pieces, cooking it, and sealing it in crocks.

Women's work in gardening increased as well. Gardening is time-consuming throughout the growing season. Unlike grain production, gardening involves a host of different plant species, which need to be planted and harvested at different times. Moreover, some garden plants need special care. Several farm women remarked, for example, that watering the tomatoes, tying up the beans, thinning overgrown plants, and dusting the potatoes against insects have always been part of their activities in the garden. In addition, weeding has to be repeated several times during the growing season. Therefore, with more and more people to be fed on the farm, gardens probably grew in size, which meant more work in preparing the soil, planting crops, weeding, watering, thinning and tying up plants, and harvesting produce. It also meant more work in preserving the garden produce. Given the different harvest times for garden crops, preserving was an ongoing activity in the summer and fall. During interviews, farm women Maureen and Olga illustrated this with the following comments:

> We did our own canning. That was done during the whole summer. It was done in between [other work] and whenever the vegetables came up [were ready to be harvested]. For example, rhubarb already comes in the spring. In the summer you have other vegetables and you do them right away. The peas come out first. They needed to be shelled and canned. With the carrots and peas, I used to can approximately fifty quarts. Then you had beans and then you had tomatoes. The tomatoes I put upstairs and can them. And cucumbers, they come later. So, we just dilled them and put them in jars in different ways. And then your beets came which I kept under the potatoes; they kept long like that. And the cabbage was picked when we were digging the potatoes. After I dug the potatoes, I cleaned the garden right off. A lot of cabbage was made into sauerkraut

in the sealers. Canning was done all day, all summer. There were the beans, peas, tomatoes in the fall, and the fruit. The women did all this work. The men were in the fields.

Because farm women were under a lot of pressure during harvest time to get the meals ready on time, they tried to prepare as many vegetables, baked goods, and meat dishes as possible in advance. The threshing event had to run as smoothly as possible, without any unnecessary delays, because it was an expensive operation and there was always the threat of an early frost, which could jeopardize the wheat crop and, thus, the farm income. It was important to "not waste a minute, for the time element was everything in threshing."[24] For farm women this meant that efficiency and punctuality in meal preparation were crucial in order to help complete the harvest as quickly as possible. Preservation of prepared foods prior to peak times was therefore necessary. Nellie McClung wrote, for example, that it "was for the threshing that sauerkraut was put up in barrels and green tomato pickles were made; red cabbage and white were chopped up with onions, vinegar, cloves and sugar, corn scraped from the cobs, and kept in stone crocks. Every sort of cake that would keep was baked and hidden."[25] Kathleen Strange, an Alberta farm woman of the 1920s, also commented on the necessity of preparatory activities in anticipation of the threshing season. She wrote that

> "seasonal" work ... was ... planned as carefully as conditions would allow. For instance, in the spring I considered the question of meat supplies for the forthcoming summer months. We did not have any ice and fresh meat was always difficult to keep. So I "put down" as much as I possibly could. Before seeding commenced, I would get the men to kill a pig, or we would purchase a quarter of beef from a neighbour. This I would "can" in glass sealers. I would cut the meat into small pieces, pack it into sealers, season it, but add no water, and then process it for the given time—some three hours or so. Pork was usually cooked and packed into crocks, then covered with boiling lard. Both these methods permitted me to place a ready-cooked meal on the table at short notice during the summer months. ... [26]

In addition to the planning and labour that took place before the harvest crew arrived, women had to do a lot of extra planning and work during the stay of the threshers on the farm. Indeed, "threshing time was a busy time for the farmer's wife, with 18 to 25 hungry men to feed, three meals and lunch each day."[27] The absence of adequate refrigeration meant that several food items had to be prepared on a daily basis or, at least, twice to three times a week to avoid spoiling. For example, potatoes were generally peeled, washed, and cooked on the day of consumption. Often farm women prepared mashed potatoes for dinner and fried potatoes for breakfast, which required the additional tasks of mashing and spicing, cutting and frying. Breakfast generally included bacon, eggs, coffee, and bread, which had to be prepared every morning. Farm women also prepared sandwiches for an 'in-between' lunch every day, which meant slicing several loaves of bread, buttering the slices, putting different fillings in them, and, finally, wrapping them into a package to be taken out to the field. In addition, meat, vegetables, and soup were prepared daily for dinner, which, when not preserved in advance, included the additional tasks of cutting, washing, and cooking. Desserts were usually puddings or pies. Since the dairy components spoil quickly, pudding had to be prepared on the day of consumption. Pies and baked goods like bread, cakes, cookies, and doughnuts, however, could usually be prepared two to three days ahead of time in fairly large batches. Kathleen Strange wrote, for example, "In the spring, and at harvest time, I baked every other day—ten loaves and a bunch of cinnamon rolls every time."[28] This was a considerable increase in her weekly workload since she baked only twice a week during the rest of the year. Her pastries usually included a number of large cakes, pies, and cookies, in addition to the bread and buns. Olga's experience with baking for the threshers was similar. She told me, "Two loaves of bread was hardly enough to feed the threshers. I bake my own bread so I used to bake fourteen loaves per week plus a number of pies. You had to plan your meals." The amount of butter made for home consumption also increased as the number of people residing on the farm grew. One farm woman told me that there were seventeen people in her family who, together, consumed one pound of butter per day. She said that her mother had to make a lot of butter to keep up with family demands. It is not surprising, then, that buttermaking for home use increased in scope when women had to incorporate the needs of hired men and threshers in their butter production. In addition to all this extra food preparation at harvest time, the dirty dishes and cutlery needed cleaning after every meal, requiring greater amounts of water and wood to heat the stove than usual. With all the men working in the field, the women were often left to carry wood and water. Jodie remarked during our interview that women had a harder time during harvest than men since the women on her farm had to haul water and wood by themselves. During threshing time, every day presented the same routine of catering to a large number of hungry farm workers, as Nellie McClung describes:

I . . . found it hard to waken up bright and ready for the day's work, but there was no time to think about personal concerns for the men had to be fed. We prepared all we could the night before and had sliced the bacon and peeled the boiled potatoes and had pans of them ready to put in the oven dotted over with pieces of butter and sprinkled with pepper and salt, and soon two frying pans of bacon were sending out their cheerful incense and another pot of eggs was set to cook. . . . The coffee was made in big blue enamel pots and there was no question of timing or measuring. There was just one rule—plenty of coffee and let it boil until the men came in. . . . The table, made as long as the size of the room allowed, was covered with oilcloth and had sugar-bowls and cream pitchers at intervals with a cruet-stand in the middle, a fine big silver affair with at least five compartments for pepper and salt, mustard, oil and vinegar in glass containers. And then there were glass pickle dishes. . . . We sliced bread, a loaf at a time, and the table had plates of baking powder biscuits and pitchers of syrup and prints of butter. . . . At noon we often had soup as well as the meat and vegetables. . . . There was a keen satisfaction in cooking for people who enjoyed their meals like these hungry men, and I loved to see the great platters of hot roast beef beginning to show the pattern, knowing that a further supply was being sliced off in the kitchen, and that big pots of mashed and buttered potatoes and turnips were ready, too, to refill the vegetable dishes, and that the oven was full of baked rice pudding well filled with raisins, and that the big white pitchers on the table were full of thick cream, and if worst came to worst, that is if they cleaned up everything, we still had the pantry shelves full of pies and a brown crock full of doughnuts.[29]

The recollections of farm women from the Rathwell area also document women's daily routines:

Get meals! You would get up at around four o'clock in the morning and start your stove. And some of those darned men would sit there and didn't even get up to dig your potatoes. They would watch you go dig your own potatoes. You had potatoes for dinner and supper and sometimes fried up for breakfast too. We had to make three meals for them a day. And when it rained like this year, you just had to feed them the same. You stayed and waited. The women had to feed them. We spent the whole day making meals. It never stopped. You rushed from one meal into the other. You finished your breakfast dishes and started to get the biscuits ready for lunch. There was never a dull moment. The kids would do the chores. Get the cows in [the barn] to milk so they would be out before the horses came in.

Annie added the following anecdote:

> I was fifteen and I worked on Mrs. Smith's farm for a month and they
> had the threshers out so she needed help. They had twenty-four men. I
> helped with the cooking. At four o'clock in the morning I was up. The
> men went to work at six o'clock. They had their breakfast. And then you
> had to make everything ready for dinner. And then you would make
> biscuits and bread ready for lunch in the afternoon and supper at night.
> They [the threshers] got a late, late supper. And then [late at night] you
> turn around and you would be dead when they left the table. But you
> would still do the dishes and set your table ready for breakfast.

In addition to the immense job of food preservation and preparation,
many farm women also laundered for the hired men on the farm. Without
running water and electricity, the increase in the volume of dirty clothing
and bed linen to be washed and ironed caused a tremendous increase in the
laundering workload. Kathleen Strange illustrated this in her autobiography: "I washed for the hired men as well as for my own family. We were
always from eight to fifteen strong, according to the time of the year, and
since most of the men worked in close contact with the soil, and with
animals, there was always an astonishing pile of extremely dirty clothing—
mountains of overalls and socks, heavy underwear and flannel shirts, not to
speak of voluminous bed linen. . . . I did not . . . iron the men's work shirts.
Each lad was allowed one good shirt a week, which I washed and pressed
for him."[30] Jodie told me that she, too, placed a limit on the number of
shirts she was willing to iron. Despite this, she still ironed twenty-three
shirts a week. Hired men living with the farm family probably also generated more cleaning chores for women. Kathleen Caswell recollected that
the growing season "was a very busy time for the women . . . as the bunk
house had to be scrubbed and ticks prepared for the extra hands."[31] The
question remains as to what extent the presence of threshers increased the
volume of housecleaning. Several sources indicated that threshers did not
sleep inside the farmhouse itself. The local history of the Minnedosa district
reported that a "caboose went along with the [threshing] outfit as it moved
from farm to farm where men slept in bunks, taking along their own blankets."[32] This sleeping arrangement must have saved farm women work during harvest time. However, some archival sources have indicated that this had
not always been the case, especially during the first few years after the advent
of the threshing machine. Kate Johnson wrote in 1888, for example, that
sleeping-cabooses "didn't travel with the threshing-outfits as they do nowadays. Instead sleeping-room was supplied by the farmer, each man usually

bringing along his own pillow and blankets for a shakedown on the kitchen floor. In our home, the owner of the machine was treated with a little more deference, and in order to provide him with a real bed the children doubled up, four sleeping in the space that previously accommodated only two."[33]

The presence of an expanded labour force on the farm generated so much extra work for farm women that the shortage of labour to do domestic work became an acute problem after 1890.[34] Yet, to run the household as smoothly as possible, a steady and reliable labour supply was as important to the farm woman responsible for domestic work as it was to her husband responsible for fieldwork. Whenever possible, female help was employed to assist the farm woman with the chores in the home and barnyard. But, as Nellie McClung, writing of the year 1895, complained, it was very difficult to get domestic help.[35] Alleviating the shortage of employable women soon became the focus of immigration propaganda. A Canadian Pacific Railway advertisement directed "To The Young Women Of England, Ireland And Scotland" announced, for example, "[While] we require twenty to thirty thousand men to assist in reaping our bountiful harvest annually, there are but few young women come to the assistance of the ladies, whose duty is to provide for their household and for the additional help."[36] Gradually, it did become easier to find domestic help. Single immigrant women, as well as young women from the newly opened frontier areas of Manitoba, of-fered their labour on the expanding farms of the south. Domestic servants were usually assigned to menial tasks. Mary told me, for example, that when she was a domestic servant, she had to do the laundry for the family that employed her and their hired help, while another girl was employed to help with meal preparation.

It appears that a hierarchy of tasks existed among women, children, and hired help. "Roughly speaking, the chores that required the least skill or organizational ability went to children (carrying water, milking cows, sim-ple mending); those that were more arduous went to servants (scrubbing floors, doing laundry, minding small children, pounding corn); but those that either required fine judgement (churning butter) or some creativity (fine sewing) or much experience (making clothes) or considerable or-ganizational skill (cooking meals) remained with the housewife herself."[37] Given the importance of planning and the need to coordinate the work of domestic servants and children, women's organizational responsibilities grew in scope as the volume of their responsibilities for subsistence production and domestic work increased.

The overall increase in the work involved in food production, preserva-tion, and preparation, as well as in laundering, cleaning, and organizational activities—caused by an expanded workforce on the farm—drew women out of fieldwork, thereby acting as a pull factor. Remarks made by farm women during interviews confirm this. In explaining why her mother did not do any fieldwork, Jodie related, for example, "Mother never worked in the field. When you have to feed seven or eight people, boy you didn't have time to be out there. No way! You have to can all the fruit and preserve the vegetables and look after the garden. That is *your* big chunk! I think that is what the women mainly did." Similarly, Frieda said, "You did not have time for field work; you had to cook for so many men."

As prosperity levels rose and food needs on the farm expanded, people acquired more draught horses, cattle, pigs, poultry, and even a special pair of horses to draw the buggy. Farm women became increasingly involved in tasks related to livestock keeping, which acted as a second pull factor drawing women out of field-crop production. I was told that keeping livestock is a lot of work. Maureen noted, for example, "You had to look after everything that was living—it was the same like a person—it needed a lot of labour and attention." Jane, too, explained that "cattle is labour intensive—it is twenty-four hours a day, 365 days of the year." Women have always been heavily involved in livestock care on the farm. In looking after the poultry flocks, they were responsible for feeding and watering the birds, rounding them up at night, cleaning the coop, collecting the eggs, setting the 'clockers' (to hatch eggs), looking after the new chicks, and so on. In summer, when farm flocks reached maximum size, women's work in poultry raising increased proportionally. Several farm women told me that their flocks numbered about 200 birds. Children generally assisted with menial tasks like feeding and watering the birds and collecting the eggs, but women retained overall responsibility and performed the more complex tasks themselves. Karen told me, for example, that looking after the farm's young chicks was always her mother's job. Young chicks need special care, she said. They have to be fed well and kept warm, and their health watched carefully. Another farm woman, keeping chickens at the time of our interview, related similarly, "I feed them and look after them when they are first on the farm when they are quite small. That is always my responsibility. I bring them in at night for the first three or four weeks." Monitoring young chicks, managing the 'clockers,' and redistributing the eggs for successful hatching requires skill based on years of experience. Women are therefore not likely to delegate these tasks to children.

In hog raising, too, women looked after the well-being of pregnant sows and young piglets. Carol related, for example, "There was lots of walking to the barn at night. Each sow got about ten young ones and you had to watch them. They were clumsy and could easily get hurt by the big sow. Delivering the piglets was heavy work. A sow would weigh two hundred or three hundred pounds and it could crash down on the piglets if you didn't push the sow over." On Helen's farm, too, the women were in charge of the sows and piglets, which included watering and feeding the animals and cleaning the pigpens. Hog raising, she explained, was part and parcel of the women's responsibility for food production on the farm. Every summer one or two pigs were slaughtered and preserved for family consumption. It appears that when hog raising became a more specialized and commercial activity after the 1940s, men became more heavily involved in this production process.

With respect to raising large livestock, however, men seem to have always been responsible for the horses and oxen on the farm, probably because these were considered an extension of their fieldwork. Husbands, fathers, and sons usually fed the horses and cattle in the morning, and cleaned out the barn once a day. Even so, women were often involved in the feeding and watering chores. In fact, one archival source reported that "a job that the men felt was a little beneath them...was pumping the water for the cattle to drink out of the well."[38] Watering large livestock was very time-consuming and generally not fondly remembered by most farm women. Maureen said, for example, "All the hours we spent watering the cattle. You thought the cattle and horses would *never* finish drinking. We had to pump it from a well, and pump and pump. Those cattle and horses just drink gallons." On her parental farm this chore was performed twice a day—in the morning and at night. In wintertime, watering was even more time-consuming. The wells and dugouts would freeze, and new strategies had to be found to get enough water for family and livestock needs. Several farm women told me that one method they used was melting snow. Another method was chopping a hole in the dugout. Jane related, "I can remember when you had to go to the dugout and chop a hole every day to let the cattle go for a drink. And if it was storming it was no nice state, because the cattle didn't like the cold any more than you did. You just turned them out and they would walk to the dugout."

Although children often participated in livestock-related chores like watering, women remained in charge of the tasks performed by them. Frieda, a mother of six, related that looking after the farm's livestock was a "family thing" but she herself "would see to it that it was done." While her children assisted her, however, she did most of the tasks involving livestock herself. One such task was producing feed. Frieda, like many of her counterparts, made hay for the horses and cattle on the farm. She said, "I didn't do much fieldwork [in regard to grain crops] but I did in haying!" Women were generally involved in mowing, raking, pitching, and stacking hay. Their participation in the various haying tasks may be explained by the fact that even with the help of a horse-drawn mower and raker, haying was slow and time-consuming. With the all-important grain harvest just around the corner, haying had to be done as quickly as possible. Time was scarce and the work was voluminous. Similar factors had caused high levels of family involvement in haying in the Red River period. It is therefore not surprising to see that even on the well-to-do farms of the late nineteenth and early twentieth centuries, men, women, and children cooperated in haymaking in an effort to get as much of the haying done as possible by the time grain harvesting and threshing commenced.

Probably the most time-consuming aspect of women's livestock-related work, however, was dairying. As the number of milk cows increased, women's dairying chores grew proportionally. Sandy told me, for example, that "there was just more work to do, everything got bigger. There was more cattle," she said, "so you had to milk more cows." Apart from having to milk more cows twice a day, one had to bring them to the barn at night and return them to the pastures after milking. This, too, was often done by farm women and their daughters and, as the recollections of Annie and Jane testify, could be very time-consuming. Annie and her mother, for example, spent whole evenings "hunting" cows to take them to the barn for milking. Jane sent her dog to the pasture to start the round-up and collected her twelve milk cows on horseback. Other farm women, too, told me about their involvement in taking cattle and often the horses as well to pasture. On farmsteads where pastures had not yet been fenced in, someone had to watch the cattle continuously to keep them out of the grain fields. As the case of young Nellie McClung illustrates, this task was often assigned to a young daughter, suggesting that female involvement carried on from generation to generation.[39]

Another factor at work in changing the division of labour between men and women on the farm was the gradual withdrawal of men from all subsistence activities. Where traditionally there had been high degree of task sharing between the spouses, women were now left with the bulk of the work. And, since the decline in men's participation in subsistence activities coincided with an increase in the number of people and livestock to be cared for on the farm, women were doubly taxed. This no doubt acted as a third pull factor drawing women out of field-crop production by placing greater demands on their time and energy in subsistence and domestic work.

Men, meanwhile, became increasingly involved in commercial activities in response to the rapidly developing cash economy. New field equipment was introduced, which made cash-crop production on a large scale possible. As the acreage under cultivation increased, the various tasks involved in the grain production grew in scope. Threshing, for example, became more time-consuming as crop size increased, placing greater demands on men's time. So did the maintenance of sophisticated field equipment, which, compared to the relatively simple hand tools of previous decades, was more difficult to repair, often requiring new parts from distant service centres. This is well illustrated in Nellie McClung's autobiography where, in a chapter aptly entitled "Men and Machines," she describes the growing demands of machinery repair.[40] She also commented on the men's growing preoccupation with equipment maintenance as Sunday, traditionally a day of rest, became the day to overhaul the threshing machine.[41] Increased farm-improvement activities also placed greater time constraints on men. Breaking new land for cultivation was a major summertime occupation.

Construction was another. Sod and log buildings, which had functioned as homes and barns in the first few years of settlement, were now replaced by frame buildings. In addition, as family farms grew in size, men built bigger houses and additional barns, cattle sheds, grain bins, and water wells. Neighbouring men often formed construction bees, which called for reciprocation, drawing husbands and sons away from their own farms. Moreover, in the early decades of community building, men participated in the construction of schools, churches, and roads, requiring their absence from the farm as well. Threshing gangs were often formed on the same reciprocal principle as the construction bees, which, once again, meant that the male members of the household were absent from their own farms while helping with threshing elsewhere. Activities commonly carried out by men during the winter months also began to demand more of their time. This, too, limited their traditional involvement in subsistence activities. Depending on the amount of grain for market and the distance from farm to elevator, grain hauling may well have been the most time-consuming task for men during the winter months. In the early 1880s, before most towns had their own elevators and railway facilities, grain had to be hauled to larger commercial centres, often far distant. In addition, given the mode of transportation of the day—slow-moving, horse-drawn wagons with a capacity of less than 100 bushels—frequent trips were necessary, making grain hauling especially time-consuming. Toward the end of the nineteenth century, when many agricultural districts became connected to the transcontinental railways through branch lines, the distance from farm to elevator decreased. Although this reduced the amount of time per trip, the quantities of wheat to be hauled had increased as farms expanded in size. The advantages of shorter distances were therefore offset by more numerous trips. Grain hauling could "occupy the entire winter."[42] A farmsteader of the time recalled in this respect, "[The] winter months were the time for hauling the wheat to market. As we were about thirteen miles distant from the nearest grain elevator, hauling the several thousand bushels of wheat was a major problem."[43]

Another of men's winter pursuits was cutting and hauling wood for construction and fuel. This was especially the case in those areas of the province where trees and bush were abundant. During one of our interviews, Henry, a retired farmsteader whose father had had a contract for as much as 200 cords of wood per winter, emphasized the amount of time that went into cutting cordwood, given that one person could cut and split only about one and a half cords per day. Cordwood hauling could also be very time-consuming, as the memoirs of late Rathwell resident Henry Gaultier illustrate: hauling just one load of cordwood, a "twelve miles round trip" with only a pair of oxen to pull the cart, "was a day's work."[44]

Yet another of men's winter activities was cutting and hauling ice blocks from nearby rivers to stock the ice house for cold storage in the summer. This was often done in the form of ice-cutting bees among neighbours, which might call the men away from their own farms for days at a time. As a result of the men's increased workload on and off the farm, women and children invested more of their time and energy in subsistence activities. A young woman of the time illustrated this development in her memoirs:

> My father and one hired man, a young Englishman, had been hauling wood from the bush six miles away every day that it was fit. Load upon load they hauled.... Laborious work but necessary. My sister and I did most of the chores to enable them to haul as much wood as possible....
> [The cattle] must be fed, watered and milked....Towards five o'clock in the afternoon my sister and I lit the lantern and did the milking and fed and watered the cows. We carried the water from the well.... Fortunately the well was not frozen. That done, we took the milk to the house.... We carried in wood and water....[45]

Where men's labour was reduced, women and children stepped up their own direct involvement. Jane, a long-time resident and farm woman of southwestern Manitoba, told me, for example, that her husband never participated in milking in the summer because of his fieldwork commitments. Without his help, Jane and her children had to spend twenty-five percent more time on milking to compensate. The gradual withdrawal of men from gardening is also evident from literary sources and interviews with farm women. One author wrote that "with the growth of commercial farming, farm operators in general became less concerned with gardening as essential to existence, and . . . farm women in general maintained varying degrees of involvement in the farm garden. . . ."[46] Likewise, many farm women told me that gardening became an almost exclusively female responsibility on the farm. The only tasks in which men continued to participate were related to preparing the garden plot for cultivation. Their assistance in other tasks such as hoeing, weeding, watering, and harvesting became minimal or disappeared altogether. Frieda, who was a young farm woman in the early 1920s, illustrated this development by saying: "We had a big garden and grew enough vegetables for a year. My husband enjoyed gardening and helped out. But that changed with time. It finally got to be *my* garden. He always cultivated it with a horse and small cultivator. I used to lead the horse and walk beside it." Frieda explained that her husband, like so many of his contemporaries, got increasingly caught up in the various aspects of commercial grain production and farm-improvement projects like breaking more land for cultivation and building a bigger house for the growing family. Increasing livestock numbers and grain crops on the farm also demanded much of her husband's time in construction activities.

With women spending more and more of their time and energy on subsistence activities and livestock-related chores, they found themselves increasingly drawn out of field-crop production. This development was reinforced by the advent of more sophisticated household appliances and wares, which had the effect of reorganizing the domestic division of labour—women came to be responsible for more of the domestic work themselves. Toward the end of the 1800s, a number of changes took place in the technological system underlying housework. New household appliances such as cookstoves, washing machines, and cream separators, and products such as canning equipment, refined flour, manufactured cloth, and coal-oil lamps, became available through local retail outlets and mail-order houses. Commercial services like butcher shops and grist mills also became accessible.

It might be deduced that the industrialization of housekeeping with the advent of new products eased the burden of women's work in the home. However, as Ruth Cowan, the author of an enlightening book on the history of housework in North America, has argued, in order "to discover whether industrialization has made housework easier [one] must ask not only whether one activity has been altered, but also whether the chain in which that activity is a link has been transformed."[47] For example, while the widespread use of cast-iron stoves reduced the tasks of cutting and hauling wood because they were more efficient burners than the open-hearths and simple box stoves of earlier times, at the same time they transformed the entire cooking work process into a more complex and time-consuming responsibility by allowing different methods of cooking to take place simultaneously. Boiling potatoes, simmering a soup, and baking a pie became possible all at once, making one-dish meals obsolete. Since the provisioning of fuel was traditionally a male responsibility and the provisioning of prepared foods a female responsibility, it becomes evident that the presence of sophisticated cast-iron stoves saved the labour of men while adding to that of women. Moreover, the cast-iron stove brought along the extra tasks of daily cleaning and weekly polishing to prevent rusting.[48]

The availability of highly refined industrial flour caused similar changes in grain processing and baking. Whereas the tasks involved in constructing grain-processing tools and grinding and bolting became obsolete, the various tasks involved in baking became highly labour-intensive. With the coarse flours of earlier times, only 'quick breads' like bannock and 'quick cakes' like scones and oat cakes had been common. An authentic bannock recipe, received during a visit to Lower Fort Garry, a museum depicting life in the Red River Settlement, calls for merely five minutes of mixing and kneading ingredients and only twenty minutes of baking. Likewise, scones required only a light tossing of ingredients and brief kneading and baking of the dough. Other pastries did not yet exist. A Red River woman of the time commented, for example, "We had no cakes or pies in those days."[49] The introduction of fine wheat flour allowed for the baking of 'yeast breads,' pastries, cakes, and other confections. The transition to baking with fine wheat flour was gradual in Manitoba, occurring at different rates in different areas of the province. Many settlers of the newly opened frontier regions, for example, ground their grain by hand and baked 'quick breads' until well into the twentieth century. Ruth, who came to Manitoba from Ukraine in 1903, told me that for many years her "mother was grinding her own flour, making brown flour from which she baked brown bread in the oven in the yard every day." The well-established settlers of Manitoba's prime farm areas, on the other hand, were already baking the lighter 'yeast bread'—probably using wild hops to make the yeast—before the turn of the century. Unlike the relatively quick baking procedures of the past, yeast breads called for the preparation of a yeast culture, heavy and frequent kneading, and lengthy periods of rising and baking. Likewise, the new cakes called for lengthy beating and mixing of ingredients to adequately aerate the batter. So, even though the adoption of industrial flour eliminated certain grain-processing tasks in which both genders had traditionally been involved, women, unlike men, did not enjoy a net saving of labour because baking had become more complex and time-consuming. Moreover, with the increase in number of people working on the farm and with the higher levels of consumption associated with greater prosperity, the baking process expanded in volume. Pies, cakes, doughnuts, and many other kinds of baked goods became daily consumption items towards the late 1800s. Most women baked twice a week, but at threshing time it was more common for them to bake every other day. Of course, on special occasions such as a picnic, wedding, funeral, or for Sunday guests, extra provisions were baked. Kathleen Strange noted that, in order to provide for possible guests on Sunday, she would bake several loaves of bread, two large cakes, numerous cookies, and at least six pies.[50]

When canning equipment became widely available in the late pioneer era, the work involved in preserving food changed dramatically. In the Red River Settlement and on the frontier, garden produce had been kept in mud basements, and fruit was generally dried into cakes. Meat, particularly pork, was cured by salting or smoking. Beef, however, was seldom cured and, as a result, could spoil quickly in the summer. Whereas many farm families of the Red River Settlement relied on pemmican, the pioneers of the late 1800s organized 'beef rings,' which allowed them to eat fresh beef on a regular basis throughout the summer. A beef ring was a cooperative arrangement among neighbouring farm families whereby, each week or month, the members took turns in contributing an animal for slaughter and distributing the fresh meat among the member households. Canning food was a great deal more time- and energy-consuming than simply storing vegetables in a mud basement, drying fruit into small clusters, or curing meat. Canning required cutting and spicing the food, and washing, sterilizing, and filling the sealers, then cooking it for proper preservation. However, it allowed women to put their meats and produce up in different ways. Fresh beef and chicken, and salted or smoked pork could now be varied with canned meats, which were prepared using various recipes. Similarly, tomatoes, beets, cucumbers, cabbage, and other vegetables could be pickled or processed into a variety of products. Fruits, too, could be preserved into jams, jellies, or various pie fillings. In addition, canning equipment enabled farm women to preserve food items that, because of their perishable nature, had not been preserved in the past. For example, eggs and certain vegetables like tomatoes or cucumbers, which had been summer and early fall foods, now became a winter and spring food choice as well. The same applied to fruits. Certain berries could be preserved by drying, though others, like strawberries and raspberries, could not. Canning fruit, therefore, allowed for the consumption of greater quantities and varieties of fruits during the entire year. Just as the cast-iron stove meant the demise of one-pot cooking, so, too, did canning result in the replacement of simple food-processing recipes with varied recipes and comparatively complex procedures. Consequently, canning triggered an increase in women's workload in food preservation. It "vastly increased the amount of work that women were expected to do when the season was 'on,'" which, no doubt, was further augmented by the need to feed an expanding work force on the farm.[51]

When commercial services became available, they, too, like many industrial products, changed the nature and balance of men's and women's work in the farm household. Butchery, for example, eliminated the traditionally male tasks of killing and cutting up livestock for family consumption. However, the role of women in meat processing and especially in preservation remained, by and large, unchanged for some time. Similarly, with the widespread introduction of factory-made cloth, tasks involving the home production of cloth, such as raising and shearing sheep, and washing, carding, spinning, weaving, and knitting wool, were reduced. On some prosperous farms they were eliminated altogether. This is illustrated by Nellie McClung's mother, who had always produced cloth herself but left her spinning wheel and loom behind in Ontario when she moved in the 1880s because she had been informed that local stores in Manitoba would sell factory-made cloth.[52] Although the decline in home production of cloth reduced the labour of men, women, and children in related tasks, women, unlike men and children, experienced not a reduction in total workload but, rather, a shift from one set of tasks to another. The adoption of factory-made cloth, especially cotton, increased the sewing, mending, and laundering tasks for which women had traditionally been responsible. Factory-made cloth was less durable than homemade wool and leather garments. This is, once again, illustrated by Nellie McClung's mother, who asserted that "hand-made cloth will wear ten times as long."[53] The lesser durability of materials like cotton increased the number of times women had to sew new garments and mend old ones. Moreover, the adoption of factory-made cloth coincided with "an increase in the amount of clothing that people expected to own."[54] As community life developed in rural Manitoba, participation in social events called for clothing to meet a dress code. Several farm women mentioned during interviews the need for school outfits and proper clothing with which to attend church and dances. The larger amount of clothes owned per person greatly expanded women's sewing workload. Larger wardrobes also meant more laundry. What is more, factory-made cloth was more easily laundered and could, therefore, be washed more often.[55] Despite the availability of washing machines, women's laundering workload did not diminish immediately. Although they eliminated the task of scrubbing and, when outfitted with a wringer, the task of wringing out the laundry by hand, they created the new tasks of 'cranking' the washing machine and wringer by hand since early washing machines were not yet automated. As pioneer woman Peggy Holmes noted, "[turning] the handle to swish the clothes around was a heavy job. . . . I always had several long skirts and petticoats to wash. . . . Our heavy underwear, thick sweaters, and Harry's work overalls and woolen socks were difficult to get clean with our primitive apparatus."[56] Also, one still had to make soap, carry fuelwood and water into the house, heat the stove, boil the water, cook, dry, iron and fold the clothes, dispose of the dirty water, and, finally, scrub the kitchen floor. Given that other tasks within laundering remained unchanged and that the numbers of garments to be laundered grew, washing machines did not greatly reduce the time that women had to invest in this job. Even the advent of gas-powered washing machines did not do so since, while cranking was eliminated, related tasks were unaffected. Water still had to be hauled, heated, and carried to the machine and, after the actual laundering task was completed, had to be disposed of. In fact, farm woman Olga indicated that until piped-in water and water heaters became available, automated washing machines increased the water-hauling task because they required more water. What is more, given the expense and complexity of automated washing machines, women tended to carry out more of the laundering tasks themselves rather than delegate the operation of the machines to inexperienced children and hired help. In addition, it appears that in accordance with the social norms of the day, women in former times ironed more items than is common today. Sandy told me, for example, that women "ironed everything, that's how it was done." The local history of Minnedosa and pioneer author Kathleen Strange, too, mentioned the ironing of "frilled petticoats, baby's long dresses and father's bosom shirts and stiff cuffs, [and] towels, sheets, pillow slips, and so forth."[57]

With the introduction of sewing machines, coal-oil lamps, and cream separators, women's domestic work load continued to expand. They became responsible for the upkeep of the glass globes (chimneys) of coal-oil lamps, involving the daily removal of soot.[58] Candlemaking, on the other hand, had involved task sharing with children and had been carried out periodically, not daily. Similarly, when cream separators replaced the shallow milk pans of the past, task sharing with children and hired help in separating cream declined. I was told during one interview that a cream separator "was a machine like a centrifuge—it turns very fast and the cream comes up because it is lighter—milk goes through a channel and is separated in different spouts." The early cream separators were cranked by hand. Later on, gas-powered ones became available. Because of the complexity and expense, women may have been inclined to operate them themselves. The operation of the gas-powered separator, especially, could be a tedious chore, as is illustrated by Florence Morrison's account of her grandmother's first cream separator, purchased in 1903: "This machine was equipped with an oil cup, similar to that on engines, a drop every few seconds, also had a clutch that would slip, so no power, then Grandma would take a lid off the back and with a little ashes on a teaspoon give it the treatment, and off it would go, to get the job finished."[59] Women also became responsible for the daily maintenance of the cream separator. One farm woman commented during an interview, for example:

> That cream separator! It had to be washed in the morning—all those little things and spouts on the cream separator. And if you didn't put them in the right order and you put the milk through in the next morning, all the milk would run over the floor if you didn't put the discs in the right order. Because you see, you had to take the separator apart, then wash it, and then put it back together again. If you did it right away [wash the separator immediately after use], it wasn't too bad, but if you let it sit, the cream and milk would settle on it and it would harden. Well, leave *that* for a couple of hours and you have these eighteen or twenty discs that all stuck together. You couldn't even pull them apart. And imagine washing *that* [the hardened milk] out of all those little grooves. And if you didn't, it would spoil the cream the next day because it tasted rotten. And another thing, that cream separator had spouts which needed to be set properly. Otherwise you would get milk in your cream or, oh God, on the floor!

Evidently, cleaning the cream separator was not only a tedious chore but a complex one as well. In the past, with the use of milk pans, almost anyone could have cleaned the separating utensils. However, children or servants were probably not always allowed to take the separator apart, clean it, and reassemble the different parts afterwards. This work fell to the farm woman herself.

While the purchase of household appliances, consumer goods, and commercial services removed the tedium of many tasks in housekeeping, it also reshaped the domestic work patterns. Contrary to common belief, it did not reduce the investment of time by women in domestic work. Even though laborious but simple tasks were now mechanized, the remaining manual tasks became more complex, and many new domestic tasks were consequently created. Because these tasks required additional skill and care, they became the responsibility of women. Also, a larger work force, greater prosperity, and a desire for higher standards of material consumption increased the scope of domestic work. For example, as homes became larger, women spent more time housecleaning. On the whole, given technological change and increasing demands, women's investment of time in domestic work increased while that of men and children declined. Indeed, "in almost every aspect of household work, industrialization served to eliminate the work that men (and children) had once been assigned to do, while at the same time leaving the work of women either untouched or even augmented."[60] The industrialization of housekeeping can, therefore, be included among the pull factors drawing women out of field-crop production.

The development of commercial grain farming with the advance of the transnational railway in the 1880s caused a shift in the traditional division of labour between men and women on the well-established farms of Manitoba. Men concentrated their energies on commercial production and their labour became increasingly associated with the rapidly developing market economy. Women, on the other hand, became increasingly drawn into subsistence and domestic activities. Task sharing between men and women declined, and, as a result, a stricter segregation of farm gender roles developed. Women no longer worked in the grain fields, while men participated less and less in all domestic and subsistence chores. Notwithstanding this stricter segregation of men's and women's work on the farm, however, there can be no doubt that their work remained complementary. Women's domestic and subsistence activities facilitated the process of farm development by enabling men to invest their time and energy in farm improvement and expansion.

Breaking newly cleared land, south of Elma, Manitoba, c. 1915 (Provincial Archives of Manitoba N9703)

Group of immigrant women and children at quilting bee (Western Canada Pictorial Index)

Cutting wheat with sickle near Stuartburn, Manitoba, c. 1918 (Provincial Archives of Manitoba N9697)

Man and wife plastering house, c. 1916 (Provincial Archives of Manitoba N9631)

3.
Farm Women's Economic Contribution to Farm Development

The High Cost of Farming

Upon settlement in the province of Manitoba, settlers needed a considerable amount of cash to establish a successful farm. On average, "each homestead unit would require a capital outlay of several thousand dollars in the period of proving up."[1] Settlers had to invest in building materials, supplies, equipment, and tools with which to clear and farm the land and establish a household. These assets were very expensive, especially given the fact that the tariff and railway policies of the time inflated their purchase price. For example, tariffs levied on, primarily, American imports were set at fifteen percent *ad valorum* in the 1870s and raised to thirty-five percent in 1883. An Ontario settler, shocked by the high start-up costs of homesteading in Manitoba, wrote to his mother in the early 1880s: "Everything costs 200 percent more than in Ontario."[2] Once established, the costs of production were also very high. For example, the railway policy forced farmsteaders to pay transportation costs on goods shipped in both directions, which placed undue pressure on their limited cash resources. For many of them, this acted as an incentive to generate higher cash incomes by expanding their cash-crop acreage under cultivation. However, expansion in itself required considerable monetary investments, involving, as it usually did, the acquisition of more land through purchase. Moreover, more land meant higher taxes and additional operating costs as more machinery and hired help were needed to run the larger farm operation. The costs of equipment, repairs, and supplies, as well as the wages for threshers and hired help, amounted to high cash outlays for farm families. Kate Johnson, a Manitoba settler of the time, illustrated the financial burden in her memoirs of 1888. She wrote, "By the time binder-twine had been purchased, threshing-bills paid, and men and horses fed, there was little left to reward the farmer for his long hours of toil. If by any chance there was a surplus, most of it went to the Machine Company as payment on the plough or binder."[3] Farm expansion was costly in another way. As commodity production began to demand more of men's and women's time in related tasks, they came to rely increasingly on purchased goods and services instead of manufacturing such items as leather harnesses, shoes, cloth, and candles themselves. Moreover, with rising standards of living, certain consumer items such as baking soda, coffee, and syrup ceased to be luxuries and gradually became family staples, thereby raising the farmsteaders' cost of living. The fact that goods and services purchased in rural towns were more expensive than those bought in larger urban centres like Winnipeg constituted an additional financial burden. Storekeepers in the Interlake region, for example, were notorious for charging high prices for low-quality goods.[4]

The increased cost of farming was evident from the high levels of indebtedness incurred by farm families of the time. In the early 1930s, for example, a large proportion of farm families was indebted to banks, land companies, machinery companies, credit societies, and merchants. According to the surveys of the Canadian Pioneer Problems Committee, thirty-five percent of Manitoba farms were mortgaged by 1931, while in the Red River Valley alone, 139 of the 150 farms that supplied financial information to the surveys reported indebtedness, averaging $5707 per farm.[5] Considering that this farm district was also the most developed area in terms of farm expansion and mechanization, it is evident that farm development did not take place without a considerable financial toll.

The financial burden of establishing and operating a farm was increased by recessions in the farm economy. Economic depressions have occurred again and again in the prairie wheat economy, always affecting income security on the farm. In Manitoba, the first commercial depression had already started in 1873 when the Mackenzie government failed to ensure the rapid completion of the Pacific Railway, and grasshopper plagues destroyed the crops. These hard times were followed by an upswing in the prairie economy in the next few years. Farmsteaders were encouraged to buy land and equipment at inflated prices, often by taking out loans at high, fixed interest rates, making them financially vulnerable and subject to cash-flow problems. Just as they attempted to deal with these problems by increasing wheat yields and, thus, their incomes, a second depression set in. Wheat prices dropped to an all-time low in 1886, and for farmsteaders "struggling with the heavy costs of building, breaking land, and buying farm machinery, this blow was severe."[6] Between 1888 and 1896, the low price of wheat and poor yields due to climatic circumstances kept farm incomes low. Fortunately, an upswing in prices for farm produce occurred in 1896, but in 1912-1913 prices for wheat dropped again while freight rates went up, putting farmsteaders in a tight, cost-price squeeze. The First World War eased the severity of this downturn somewhat by creating a higher demand for wheat, leading to better prices. But benefits were quickly offset by the ever-climbing costs of production, and "in this race of rising prices and costs lay the possibility of disaster for the farmer, urged to produce to the limit and driven to increase his outlay in order to do so."[7] Immediately after the war, prices for farm produce fell again and a new upswing in the prairie economy did not occur until after 1924. Confident that prices would remain high, farmsteaders put more and more land into wheat production, which, by the late 1920s, had created an enlarged wheat supply in excess of the actual domestic and international demand. Those who relied on this cash crop as their main source of income found themselves vulnerable when prices dropped in the 1930s. The combination of low prices and severe drought conditions proved devastating for many of them.

The cyclical fluctuations in grain prices made earning an adequate income to support family and farm uncertain. This was so especially in the marginal farm areas of Manitoba where, unlike the prime farm areas, field-crop production was less readily expanded and soil productivity lower, resulting in lower farm incomes to begin with. To cope, farm families across the province relied on income from sources other than grain sales. They also attempted to stretch their income by minimizing cash outlays for family needs. As household managers, women were at the helm of these economizing efforts and carried out a variety of entrepreneurial activities on the side to generate extra income.

Women's Economizing Strategies

Farm women employed numerous strategies to economize on cash outlays. They upheld an ethic of frugality in expenditures for family needs, postponed the purchase of household appliances, provided services themselves instead of purchasing them, utilized country provisions such as wild plants and game, and, finally, maintained subsistence production for family provisioning.

In a study of Saskatchewan farm women, author Seena B. Kohl noted that the "role the woman plays in controlling family expenditures and family consumption wants . . . is important in the success or failure of the development process of the enterprise."[8] This statement applies equally well to the farm women of Manitoba, where economizing on household expenses was reinforced by an ethic of frugality in which working hard and saving diligently were high priorities. Nellie McClung's complaints about her mother's 'penny pinching' illustrate this. Despite the fact that her family's farm was prospering, her mother continued to insist on economizing on certain types of luxuries. "Even in the face of an abundant crop, the acid little economies of the household went on, little restrictions which burned into me. . . . Looking back, I can see how unfair I was to mother . . . she knew how slowly money came, with eggs ten cents a dozen and butter eighteen."[9] The same attitude was also illustrated by the mother of Kate Johnson. "When the prices of wool, butter and eggs had been ascertained and the amounts totalled up, so that she knew how much money she had to spend, mother's shopping-list was brought out. . . . Not until all the necessary articles on her list were struck off did mother indulge in luxuries, and even these were carefully selected."[10]

The need for frugality affected the purchase of household appliances as well. The industrialization of housekeeping usually lagged behind the process of farm mechanization. This did not change even in the post-war era, despite relative prosperity on the average farm. Basswood farm woman JoAnn remarked during an interview that, "even though technology came in after the war, *who* made use of the technology first? The men! Not the women! I know women who, for years, didn't have waterworks in the house when the water was in the barn. I don't know why it was so necessary for these cows to be so well looked after. But I suppose from the men's point of view, they could do their work faster and it was better for the animals so they would grow wool faster or get fatter faster; so they [the men] could sell it faster; they felt that the farm was where the income was coming from." This reasoning was also expressed by other farm women. Maureen, whose family had farmed near Miami, told me that "farm mechanization was more important because that was where your money and food was coming from; the mechanization of the home was of second-rate importance." She added, "It only made sense that they replaced the horse. A horse is a living thing and you could only work it so much, so many hours a day. It would be foolish to have a washing machine in the house and trying to work with horses outside. So, it [farm mechanization] was just economy wise. You could cover more land and put in more grain." This situation was not unique to Manitoba. Seena Kohl noted that farm women in southwestern Saskatchewan were also "willing to delay the accumulation of household aids."[11] Especially in families with one or several sons, women supported farm expansion "with its necessary contraction of domestic consumption."[12] Other authors have also commented on women's economizing attitudes. One source explains, for example, that people were chronically short of cash with which to buy manufactured goods. As a result, they had to keep their purchases to a minimum by producing everything they could at home, whether it was a pound of lard or a cake of soap. In many cases, they had to do without expensive labour savers like washing machines and running water. The settlers' first priority was not comfort but economic security: their future depended on making a commercial success of the farm. And any extra money was less likely to be spent on household conveniences than on efficient machinery for producing the cash crop. Consequently . . . long after the farm work had been taken over by horses and machines, many farm homes ran on womanpower.[13]

By putting off the purchase of domestic technology and thus maintaining more labour-intensive procedures, women made an indirect, yet vital, contribution to the development of the commercial component of the farm.

As noted, farm women provided a host of services for farm and family that were aimed at economizing on farm and household expenses. Carol told me, for example, that she used to save money by looking after the livestock's health. She said: "We treated the pigs ourselves. I used to watch the vet at work and learn from him. Later I would do it myself and that saved about $85 for a vet's visit. A vet is too expensive, especially when the animal dies anyway. Even if you sold that pig later, you did not get that expense out!" Similarly, Mae Olstad related: "They used to call me the veterinary. I never learned from anybody. I just wasn't afraid and I just didn't have the money."[14] Many farm women also restrained family expenses on medical services. Although women generally delivered children without the help of a doctor in pioneering times when professional medical assistance was lacking, they often continued to do so in later times to save money. For example, Beatrice Vincent related:

> [We] sent for [a doctor] and they was three hours late and I had everything done, had the baby dressed and myself washed and the afterbirth taken out and put into the heater. And then he came and felt my pulse and said, "Well you're just as nature led you. That's forty-five dollars please." Yes, that was it and he'd only come six miles. . . . But I had sent for him and naturally I had to pay him. So after that when I was in a family way I never sought for any doctor. I asked the Lord to help me and he gave me health and strength. I had all twelve of them without any doctor. . . .[15]

Women commonly assisted each other as midwives during childbirth and saved on doctors' bills in this way. They also continued to manufacture home remedies for a variety of illnesses, even after patent medicine became available through travelling salesmen and local stores at the turn of the century. Women frequently shared their medical knowledge in an attempt to save money and still cure their families. For example, with respect to birth-control remedies, a letter from a daughter to her mother revealed: "So you wanted some information. Well, I can tell you several methods. I have the real recipe of that cocoa butter . . . a friend's . . . sister . . . got from her doctor after she'd had four. He charged her $50 for it, but since, she's given it to dozens and it works."[16] Cash was saved by providing one's own dental care as well. For example, Peggy Holmes described how a neighbouring farm woman pulled her own and probably her children's teeth in an attempt to economize on such expenses.[17] Many women also provided hair-cutting services for their families. During an interview with Jennifer, she recalled that in the 1920s and 1930s, when she was a young girl, "all the hair cutting was done by mother." Similar comments were made about women's clothes manufacturing, which was also aimed at restraining family expenditure. Frieda remarked, for example, "Women ordered clothes from Eatons. It certainly did make life easier for women, but, of course, you still bought material to sew and yarn to knit. You didn't buy everything ready-made just because it was in the catalogue! You couldn't afford that! Shoes, you got them the same way as cloth [through the catalogue] but I sometimes made shoes for the little ones." Likewise, Meg, a retired farm woman from the Swan River district, related: "I bought material from Eatons through the catalogue from Winnipeg, for a few dollars. And, then, *you* make everything: boys' underwear, boys' pants, boys' shirts, socks. You don't go and buy, you *make* everything!" Many families economized further by sharing clothes and altering hand-me-downs. This was so especially with children's clothes and shoes. Annie told me, "[In the 1920s and 1930s] I used to get clothes given to me and cut them down and make them all for the kids." Joan related in the same vein, "I always did my own sewing. 'Necessity is the mother of invention,' and I altered clothes, especially winter coats. I always altered hand-downs for the kids. We were always able to cope."

The use of flour and sugar bags and second-hand materials was an additional economizing strategy. During a group interview, farm women from the Red River Valley area recalled, "[During the 1920s and 1930s] we used flour bags to make pillowcases, sheets, teatowels, diapers, children's underwear and baby's sheets. You had to get the print [lettering] out first and then bleach it to make it white, or dye it to get a colour." An interview with a group of retired farm women from the Rathwell area yielded similar comments. "But look at the things we used to make out of flour bags.

And we had to rub and scrub those things to get the print out first. Sheets and pillowcases we made, and teatowels, slips and even bloomers. Yes, it wasn't funny." In the marginal farm areas, the use of this economizing strategy went beyond undergarments and linen, and included outergarments as well. In addition, materials produced on the farm, such as wool and hemp, were used as much as possible to reduce spending. The local history of Fisher Branch contains a number of family histories that illustrate this. For example, the family history of Polly Hnatiuk, who raised ten children between the 1920s and 1940s, revealed: "Most of the clothes were made at home from dyed or bleached flour and sugar bags. These home-tailored garments included everything from underwear to 'Sunday best.' Wool was carded by hand, and yarn was spun on spinning wheels. This yarn was used for knitting stockings and mittens for the whole family."[18] In another family history, Annie Huta recalled how she coped with the need to clothe six children between the 1920s and 1950s. "If anybody had hard times, we sure did. ...We barely had enough to live on. I used to knit all the socks, sweaters, and scarves for all the children. I sewed clothes from printed flour bags; the white flour bags I used to dye red, yellow, and blue, and make shirts or dresses."[19] Henry mentioned during an interview that his mother manufactured overalls and shirts out of sugar bags because bag material was "sturdier for heavy cleaning and livestock tasks." Work clothes had to be manufactured frequently and the use of sugar bags avoided expenditures on store-bought clothing materials, especially when cash was hard to come by. The use of flour and sugar bags for outergarments to be worn in public places like schools or churches indicates the severity of financial hardships in the marginal areas and the lengths to which women went to save on expenditures. Jodie of Niverville, a prosperous farm area, confirmed this. She noted, "The 1930s were bad times but my family wasn't as bad off. We used sugar and flour bags for teatowels, but some people used them for clothing."

Yet another economizing strategy employed by farm women across the province was the use of feathers for making pillows and comforters. Several farm women from the Red River Valley area related: "We made our own pillows out of sugar sacks and feathers of geese and other fowl." Michael Stasyshyn from Stuartburn recalled, " We went hunting... wild ducks. This was a great help for we had meat and mother plucked the ducks and we had feathers to make pillows."[20] Women economized by making quilts as well. "The quilts were mostly made of leftovers, scraps from dresses and aprons or of heavy patches taken from worn out trousers, suits or even underwear. ...The interlining was often of sheep's wool grown on the farm and prepared ahead of time."[21] Moreover, by pooling their labour in cooperative bees like feather-plucking and quilting bees, farm women were able to economize on commercial services when carrying out big jobs like plucking dozens of birds. For example, several farm women from the Red River Valley area told how they did things together in groups: "Like, when we plucked the turkeys and geese. The neighbours would come and help or you would go there. We had turkey-picking bees and everyone would go there. The feathers were used for pillows or comforters." Although many farm women recalled the "fun times" experienced at the various bees, co-operation between women in the manufacture of essential subsistence needs was of utmost importance in bolstering the family standards of living in both good and bad economic times. For example, on pioneer farmsteads in Minnedosa, "[winters] were cold and the log houses not too warm so much warm bedding was needed. The women ... gathered as soon after the noon meal as possible, some even coming in the morning to help 'set up' the quilt."[22] In the same fashion, farm women organized chicken showers to help new settlers economize on the expense of starting a poultry flock and help out those who had lost their flock to frost or predation. Even today, cooperative arrangements exist. For example, Nancy and Olga told me that, like themselves, many farm women still cut and wrap beef or pork together or organize pie-baking bees for big events like weddings and funerals instead of relying on the expensive services of butchers and bakers. Seena Kohl has noted that farm women in Saskatchewan form informal groups or "work exchanges" on the same basis and that this "neighboring" serves "an impor-tant function in a region were the cash for labor is in short supply."[23]

The provisioning of goods and services by farm women, whether car-ried out individually or cooperatively, was aimed at economizing on house-hold expenses and maintaining family standards of living. A related service in this respect was helping in the field when hired help was unaffordable. Women's participation in field-crop production economized on labour expenses when farm income was low. This was so especialley in the mar-ginal areas of the province where lack of income to hire help was a chronic problem. In fact, this lack of income generally forced husbands and teenaged children to seek employment off the farm, leaving women with the bulk of the farm work. Historical sources document this. For example, the local history of Fisher Branch reported that in the "summer the men hired out for threshing. . . . The women stayed home, cutting grain with a sickle, tying sheaves with bands of grain, later hauling and stacking them neatly in the yard."[24] Similarly, the local history of Pine River recorded: "When the set-tlers arrived here they had very little or no source of income. The men and older children went to work wherever there was a job."[25] One homesteader recalled, "Dad . . . left mother with the children on the farm. She had to look after the farm by herself, as the children were too small to help."[26] Several farm women from the Riding Mountain area told me that they, too, carried out fieldwork under these circumstances. They described the tasks they performed and how their labour contributed to the farm operation. Helen related that lack of money to hire help not only necessitated her fieldwork involvement on her own farm but also on that of her parents-in-law. She said: "I drove the tractor and I drove the binder. I stooked too. We worked half a section; one quarter was ours and the other quarter was [my husband's] dad's. After [my husband] finished cutting our quarter, he went to his dad's land to cut. Then I had to stook our quarter. I *had* to do that. Nobody else was there to help. [My husband] also used to leave a truck full of grain by the granary and he went threshing for his dad. And I had to empty that whole truck into the granary with a shovel. I also had to pitch sheaves during threshing time if there weren't enough men around." In addition to the family's not being able to afford hired help, the employment of Helen's husband off the farm to earn extra income meant that she often had to do more than her share of the farm work, which included looking after all the livestock. This was also the case with her daughter, Doreen, who told me that she did a lot of the fieldwork when her husband was away. "We couldn't hire someone, so I had to do it." When she married her husband in the early 1960s, she did "whatever needed to be done: stone picking, stooking, threshing, pitching sheaves, and haying." Like Doreen and her mother, Helen, farm women Olga and Carol have always had to participate in all commercial aspects of the farm because they couldn't afford hired help and their husbands were often absent from the farm. They farmed actively until the early 1980s, when their husbands' regular pension cheques allowed them to become semi-retired. Olga related the following about her direct involvement in fieldwork:

> He [her husband] was cultivating and harrowing [to prepare the land for seeding] and I used to bring out the grain [seed] with the tractor and the box [to the field]. And I used to mix the fertilizer in the grain in the [seed] drill because we didn't have a fertilizer attachment. He used to cut [the grain] with a binder since we got married. And I used to stook. We also cut for his brother and I don't know how many other places. After stooking we threshed. I was with him. I was the pitcher. And I was pitching for his brother and for another guy. I was their best pitcher! Pitching was done by fork, you had to put the sheaves on the rack. So, for about twenty different falls in a row I was threshing with the men. We threshed with one outfit and then with another. I drove the tractor and hauled

[straw] bales and, then, I would come home to do the chores [milking cows and feeding pigs], or I would do them in the morning and go out threshing. We threshed until fifteen years ago [1970]. We didn't have our own outfit. His brother had it [together] with this neighbour. [When we worked on their farms] we weren't making money; we were just working off our threshing bill. I always helped outside first and leave the inside work, because it is inside. I helped with the outside work because that is more important. He owes me a lot because I helped with everything. He always says "I did it," but we always did it [farm work] together.

Olga's farm labour economized on operating expenses in many ways. Apart from saving the wages otherwise paid to hired help, her participation helped pay off the threshing bill in kind rather than in cash. In the case of Carol, almost all fieldwork was done by her alone. Carol's husband, Tom, who participated in part of the interview, related that between 1946 and 1961 he "worked in construction." He would come home only every other weekend, leaving his wife in charge of the farm. Carol recalled the following about this period in her life: "While Tom worked in construction I farmed on my own. After the kids were sleeping I used to plough and everything for him, often until three in the morning. I often took the kids with me to the field during the day as well. When Tom came home on the second weekends, he'd do the odds and ends on the farm. He would plough the ends [corners] in and he straightened out things."

The examples illustrating women's fieldwork participation in the marginal areas contrast sharply with the earlier mentioned decline in women's fieldwork participation in prosperous areas. Yet, it should be kept in mind that even in these areas women had to perform tasks related to field-crop production from time to time. At a group interview in Rathwell, several farm women told me how they had worked as young daughters and wives in the grain and hay fields. Especially during the 1920s and 1930s when "you couldn't afford to hire help," farm women participated in various tasks related to grain production to economize on labour expenses. Annie remembered hauling grain and putting it in the granaries after she married in 1925. Her peer, Donna, also recalled hauling grain while Sandy, who was a young girl during the Depression, recalled: "We had no hired help. The family did everything. Mother never worked with the threshing machine in the field but she made hay. We all did. And we all stooked out in the field too. Dad did the seeding, but we helped to clean the seed. That was done at home with a cleaning mill that you had to turn the handle all day." Farm women from the Red River Valley area also stressed that during the 1930s, "women helped with everything, especially stooking." Some had helped with harrowing and mowing, and I was told that during the Second World War, women continued to work in the fields because there were so few males to run the field equipment. The major difference between women's field labour in the prime and marginal areas was that, in the prime areas, women's work in fields was generally limited to periods of economic recessions. In the marginal farm areas, on the other hand, women's fieldwork participation remained crucial on an ongoing basis. In either case, however, they served as a labour reserve on the farm. Their fieldwork helped economize on labour expenses when saving income was of utmost importance in making ends meet.

By making use of the free resources of nature, women were able to provide their families with certain necessities without drawing on family income. This, too, was an important economizing strategy. We already saw how, on the early pioneer farms, families relied on the utilization of country provisions such as wild fruit and game to supplement subsistence items produced on the farm. It was an essential component of the overall survival strategy of settlers. In the marginal farm areas where many families suffered from chronic cash shortages, this strategy continued to be used as a means of economizing on household expenses long after the pioneer period had come to an end. Country provisions helped them cope with otherwise low standards of living. This is particularly evident from the family history of the Obzarskis, who settled, with little money, in the Interlake region in 1908:

> Covers [for beds] were made with a filling of feathers from the prairie chickens, which were killed for meat....For food, prairie chicken and rabbits were the main meat for summer, with moose and deer meat in winter. . . . Salve was made from the gall and lard of the animals killed. Skunk lard was the best healer....A special treat was high-bush cranberries which were abundant in the woods. They were cooked, and when sugar was available, were made into jam. . . . Mushrooms were pickled in crocks in a vinegar mixture for added variety in the meals. Dandelion wine was made by most people. . . . Soap was made from the fats from deer, moose, etc., mixed with lye....Until people began to raise sheep, no one had any wool to be spun and knitted, so, of course, no one had socks or stockings to wear ... [so] tanned rabbit skins were wrapped around the feet.[27]

In many farm families, game and fowl were staple foods consumed on a daily basis and prepared by women in different ways so as to add variety to the diet. As one prairie youngster recalled, "One of our main dishes was rabbits. There was fried rabbit, stewed rabbit, rabbit ground into hamburger, smoked rabbit and rabbit everywhere, winter or summer."[28] When acute cash shortages forced men to find off-farm wage labour, a situation common in the marginal areas, women caught game themselves. For example, the family history of Pine River residents Ewan and Maria Nakonechny documents the following: "Ewan used to walk for miles to try and get work to earn money leaving Mary to take care of the children and do the chores. Mary would catch rabbits and prairie chickens for food to feed her family."[29] By using wildlife for family consumption, women were able to maintain the well-being of the farm household through high-quality nutrition while at the same time they minimized the spending of cash on dietary essentials like meat. They also minimized the expense of replacing livestock because the use of wildlife for food reduced the need to slaughter farm animals. As one local history reported: "Cattle were too valuable for milk and as oxen to be used for food....Fortunately there was no closed season on prairie chicken, wild duck and rabbit."[30] In addition to supplying traction and being valuable as producers of items for family subsistence needs, such as milk, eggs, and wool, farm livestock represented a capital asset in that the sale of livestock or livestock products generated cash and other material resources. Therefore, by supplying the farm household with wildlife products rather than livestock products, women made an additional economic contribution to the farm. While feeding their families on rabbit and fowl, and making garments out of various furs, they were able to retain their livestock products for sale. On financially strapped farms, this was essential in making ends meet.

Even farmsteaders in prime areas who had reduced their reliance on country provisions with rising prosperity levels returned to this economizing strategy when recessions set in. Numerous farm women mentioned eating wild fruits during the Depression of the 1930s, when commercial fruits like apples, oranges, bananas, or raisins were luxuries. Store-bought fruits could be had only when the family budget allowed for such expenses, I was told. Annie, whose family farmed near Rathwell at the time, explained how women used the various wild fruits to make jams, jellies, and pies. She said, "We did a lot of wild fruit picking and preserving. Cranberries and chokecherries for jelly. Also wild raspberries and strawberries. Saskatoons, too. We used to preserve them and put them in sealers. And another thing I did; instead of raisins, because you couldn't buy [afford] them, I put the saskatoons in the cake instead of the raisins." Even so, for many farm women the utilization of country provisions has been an ongoing economizing strategy until the present day. This is particularly the case with women who live on marginal farms and who have grown up with a tradition of economizing on household needs to make ends meet. For example, Mary and Olga, both of whom farm on the southern slopes of Riding Mountain, continue to make pies and jams from wild fruits, even now that a greater variety of fresh and canned fruits have become available through local stores. Another informant, Carol, a farm woman from the Interlake, told me that hunting and fishing still provide important dietary supplements on her family farm. She cleans the wild fowl and large game, and prepares the meat for the freezer or processes it into sausages. She smokes, pickles, or makes breaded patties from fish. A lot of the fish, wild fowl, and large game is preserved for winter use, which, she remarked, keeps her domestic expenses down considerably.

In the early decades of commercial farming, the continuing production of items on the farm for family subsistence was also an important means of economizing on household expenses. Frieda, who was ninety-two at the time of our interview, explained that subsistence production in the early 1900s was necessary since there was a shortage of cash. "People didn't have cash," she said. "They just made do." She stressed that meat and other food-stuffs were rarely purchased. Helen noted similarly that, in the summer-time, people rarely ate meat. Instead, they ate cream, cottage cheese, and eggs. Farm livestock, she said, was too precious to slaughter, and meat was too expensive to purchase. There is no doubt that women played a key role in economizing through subsistence production. Mary told me, for exam-ple, that the coming of stores carrying basic consumer items did not change her baking, dairying, canning, and sewing routines. She continued to pro-duce all family food products on the farm herself. Like Mary, farm woman Olga has always produced all family food products on the farm. She told me that she has never spent any money on buying poultry products, beef, pork, milk, butter, cheese, bread, or vegetables. In fact, Olga, like most farm women of her time, not only continued to provide items to meet subsist-ence needs for her family, but stepped up her food-provisioning efforts to meet the needs of a growing farm workforce as well. She raised no less than 200 chickens a year, just to feed family and threshers.

Family provisioning has always been particularly important in times of economic downturns. It helped secure family survival when farm income from commercial pursuits was lacking. Several farm women who experi-enced the 1930s vividly recalled the economic hardships and asserted that the production of items to meet subsistence needs on the farm enabled their families to "ride out the bad times." One Rathwell woman in par-ticular noted, "The trouble was that there was so much work and you didn't get nothing for it! You had to work hard just to eat three meals a day; we were short on cash. But, you had all your fresh vegetables. Once winter came, you ate up what you had canned. You couldn't afford to buy anything like that." Meg, a farm woman from the Swan River Valley, recalled similarly, "When the Depression came, we had something to eat, like milk and potatoes." She fed her family of seven children from her garden, in which she grew pumpkins, corn, beets, carrots, rhubarb, tomatoes, and potatoes. She also made her own butter and raised her own chickens, ducks, and some pigs for family consumption. Women like Meg played a crucial role in filling family needs without drawing on cash income. Moreover, by meeting the additional subsistence needs of farm labourers, women's provisioning activities further contributed to the financial well-being of their farms by minimizing the spending of farm income.

Women's Income-Generating Activities

Farm women employed numerous strategies to generate income as well. They sought employment on a wage or contract basis, they marketed country provisions and a variety of farm products, and they engaged in a number of cottage industries.

During several interviews, farm women mentioned having worked for pay to earn extra income when times were particularly hard. Invariably, these women came from marginal farm areas. Ruth, who farmed on the southern slopes of Riding Mountain, related how, after her marriage in 1913, she used to hire herself out for twenty-five cents a day to plaster homes and tend gardens. Together with her husband, she also used to "pile brush and clear land for seven dollars per acre." Gina, who farmed on the eastern slopes of Duck Mountain, used to supplement family income from the farm and her husband's off-farm job by doing "farm work for fifty cents a day." Similarly, Julia Ruta, who farmed near Cook's Creek in southeastern Manitoba, related, "Often I used to leave the children in the neighbour's care and went hoeing for farmers in Oakbank. I would earn $1.00 a day, but often, less."[31] In general, it appears that the most likely group of female household members to seek off-farm employment were teenaged daughters. Female heads of households were less likely to do so because of labour constraints at home.

Another income-generating strategy, often used in combination with working off the farm, was the sale of country provisions. Many farm women used country provisions not only for economizing purposes but for earning extra cash as well. Annie told me, for example, "The women used to get pails and pails of saskatoons. Great big milk pails, and we'd sell them for a dollar per pail. The ones you didn't sell, you'd can them." Similarly, women who utilized game for family consumption often prepared the skins for sale when cash was needed urgently. Henry, whose mother processed jack rabbits into stews and patés, told me that his mother sold the skins to earn extra income. Wild fruits and skins were usually bartered or sold at the local store for goods, during the pioneer era. The Hrynkiw family of the Pine River area "exchanged [wild berries] at the store for yards of material which were made into dresses."[32] Olga recalled likewise, "When I was still at home, I knew a woman, well, even my mother took raspberries to the store." The local history of Fisher Branch reported that hides were traded at the local store.[33] Similarly, the family history of Pine River's first storekeeper noted, "We traded fur skins, eggs and butter from customers in exchange for household supplies and clothing."[34] Some farm women also sold their products to private customers. For example, the women who lived in the Gimli district sold fresh, wild fruit to tourists in the summer resorts along Lake Winnipeg.[35] During the 1930s, the income derived from selling country provisions remained a crucial supplement to other income. This is evident from the family history of Ann Zembiak. "Life was not easy as the depression years had set in and money was extremely scarce. Ann continued to strive for survival by picking wild raspberries and selling them at one dollar per pail. . . ."[36] Farm women from the Rathwell area, too, related that they and their mothers sold wild fruit during the 1930s when farm income was particularly low.

Whereas the sale of wild fruit and skins boosted family income when extra cash was needed, the sale of cordwood and seneca roots, on the other hand, was the mainstay on many farms in the marginal areas where these resources were usually available in abundance. Contrary to the common notion that only men cut, split, stacked, and hauled cordwood, women were heavily involved in the cordwood industry as well. Two examples from the local history of Fisher Branch in the Interlake illustrate the cooperation between spouses. First of all, the family history of Anastasia Antonchuk reported, "Dad and Mom had to work very hard cutting cordwood, which they exchanged for food and clothing for the family. . . . My parents were still cutting cordwood [after several years], as this was their only means of income for the sugar and flour which had to be bought."[37] Likewise, the family history of the Lutys notes, "Mr. Luty and his wife always cut cordwood during the winter months in order to earn a few extra dollars to buy groceries. Mrs. Luty would help load and when her husband would take the cords home or to deliver them to the dealer, she would stay behind and cut more cordwood."[38] Interviews with women from various marginal farm areas revealed similar evidence. Olga, of the Riding Mountain area, told me, for example, how she assisted her husband in making cordwood. "I helped him to take the wood out; hauling from up north. He was eighteen years in the bush. For four months of every winter I was alone here. He'd come home on a Saturday and go back on Sunday. I split wood by moonlight, after all other chores were completed. I always made sure I had that pile of wood split he had sawed before he left. It had to be done by spring and he was only home on the weekends so I did it." In the marginal pockets of prime farm areas, cordwood cutting was also an important income-generating activity. Here, too, women participated, as the history of the relatively poor French settlers near Notre Dame de Lourdes illustrates:"The men worked in the bush and the women drew the wood to town with oxen. They worked hard piling and unpiling and then they knitted coming and going, most times walking behind the load."[39] Many farm families depended heavily on the sale of cordwood during the 1930s when prices for farm products were depressed. In the marginal areas, where the effects of the Depression were harshest, men and women intensified their cordwood-cutting activities to survive a declining farm economy. For example, "[D]uring the 'dirty thirties,' Riding Mountain was known as Cordwood Town."[40]

Many of the families who cut cordwood in the winter as an income-generating strategy dug seneca roots in the summer to augment income. The family history of the Malenchaks, who farmed in the Interlake region, reported, "[In] winter, the men, with wives helping, cut cordwood and hauled it to be sold in town. In summer, all spare time was spent digging seneca roots at twenty-five cents a pound."[41] Seneca roots were usually sold at the local store to obtain ready cash. In some instances, the income earned could be quite considerable. The family history of Mr. and Mrs. Lewycky documents that they "picked seneca roots and berries which they sold and saved the money to buy a farm."[42] Digging seneca roots was often a family activity in which husband, wife, and children participated together. Olga told me, for example, "We dug seneca roots for a living back home. I did and my mother did. We had a bag around the waist; the whole family, my dad and all my sisters too." However, there are numerous examples of women carrying out the work involved in digging and marketing seneca roots by themselves, without the aid of men. The local history of Fisher Branch contains several family histories that refer to this. For example, Mary Kalyta recalled, "My husband kept on clearing land and I went digging seneca roots. Once I sold my roots for sixty-six dollars. That was a lot of money."[43] Mrs. Jaman from Sirko in southeastern Manitoba recalled similarly, "[In some years] we would run short of flour. Once when my husband started haying, I left the smaller children in the care of the older girls and went seneca root picking to earn some money. Another woman and her daughter and I went several miles across the Canadian-U.S.A. line and dug seneca roots. We packed them into bags and they made a heavy load as they were green.... I took the roots to the store and was able to get two bags of flour, some sugar, salt and soap in trade. This lasted us for about two weeks and I had to go back again to get more roots."[44] There is little doubt that the two most important country provisions in Manitoba were cordwood and seneca roots. During times when farm income was minimal or absent altogether, the sale of such land-based products was often the mainstay. In fact, in many of the marginal farm areas of the province, income generation through the marketing of country provisions continued until well into the present century.

During the early years of farm commercialization and in times of depression when farm income from wheat was minimal, the sale of a variety of farm products like vegetables, poultry, eggs, wool, honey, and milk proved to be another important source of income. This was especially the case on less prosperous farms in marginal areas. Women played a major role in producing and marketing the products of mixed farming. One historical source on prairie women noted that "[the] sales of her poultry, butter and eggs were often an important source of income during the first debt-burdened seasons on a homestead, and one of the few reliable sources for years to come."[45] Another historical source on Manitoba's agricultural development indicates that "[in] many cases, eggs and dressed poultry, along with dairy butter, were used by farm wives in barter for goods obtained in country-town and village stores."[46] Women often deliberately intensified their subsistence activities to produce a surplus for income-generating purposes.

The relative distance to domestic markets played an important role in these marketing activities. For example, in the early decades of this century, Interlake pioneer women who lived near Gimli benefitted from a nearby market in the summer resorts at Lake Winnipeg. They "delivered their garden produce, cream, butter and poultry, and sold these goods to the 'campers.' They brought their goods in wagons drawn by oxen or buggies pulled by one horse. Those who lived farther away continued to bring their produce by carrying huge bundles on their backs. Young children, boys and girls, assisted their mothers in carrying quart jars of berries, baskets of eggs and pails of new potatoes."[47] And, "[farm] women who lived closer to town were able to deliver their produce fresh and cool to the steady customers they had. Most of the women delivered their produce bi-weekly: on Wednesdays and Saturdays. . . . As farmers acquired horses, they [women] drove into Gimli and other summer resort places for a distance of ten miles and more."[48] Through her marketing activities, "the farmer's wife was able to improve the farm income to a marked degree."[49] Farm families who lived near Gimli "were doing better as they were closer to markets where they could sell their farm produce."[50] In contrast, families who did not have local markets nearby, and did not own draught animals to make remote markets accessible, had much higher rates of farm failure. Women's incomes from marketing farm products were therefore essential in making ends meet on the farm. This was the case not only in the Interlake region. Examples from across the province demonstrate the crucial role played by women's financial contributions. Mary Bazay related, for instance, "[My husband and I] saved money and in 1919 bought an eighty-acre farm north of Dauphin for $1,800, paying $600 down and taking a mortgage. . . . The interest rates on our mortgage were so high that the payments and the taxes took all our earnings. When the hens started laying, I used to take a few dozen eggs to the store and buy some groceries."[51]

Mary Bazay's income-generating activity, selling eggs, helped secure the farm title by contributing indirectly to paying off the mortgage. It also safeguarded her family's standard of living, given their severely limited disposable income. Like Mary Bazay, Frieda's cash contributions through the sale of poultry products were essential in supporting farm and family. She told me that during the ten years after her marriage in 1914, she and her husband paid off the purchase price of the farm. Later on, in the 1930s, Frieda's marketing activities were still very important in making ends meet on the farm. She related:

> We worked together on the farm. It was just a ten-year contract and we managed to pay each year. We bought the farm in ten years. We had eggs and chickens which was almost our main thing for a while, because we only had this quarter section so we couldn't have a lot of cattle [to make a living with]. We had three hundred hens or so. We had an incubator which we called the "little grey hen" and kept it indoors. We experimented with it. It was just a tub-size with a lamp in the center and it held about fifty eggs. We kept the incubator in the bedroom because you had to watch the lamp. We had a utility room in which we kept the small chicks. We did not do this in wintertime; mostly in summertime when the roads were open and the storekeeper would take our eggs in. We also sold fryers. I killed and cleaned them. I sold them for twenty-five cents

each in the 1930s. It was just a little cash, yet it made a difference. My
husband didn't help with the cleaning; he drew the line there.

Apart from earning cash through the sale of poultry products, Frieda also
sold her surplus vegetables on occasion and bartered her surplus butter at
the country store for groceries. In later years she sold small amounts of
cream. Although she commented that grain sales financed the farm, it is
nevertheless evident that the income from selling dressed poultry, eggs, and
a few other farm products indirectly financed the purchase of the farm.
With Frieda's income paying for all household needs, the grain returns
could be invested in paying off the debt.

Other examples of women's financial contributions to farming include
the sale of hogs and cattle in order to meet immediate cash needs when tax
payments came up or when threshing and other operating bills were due.
Since farm women were involved in the raising of large livestock, their role
in this income-generating activity is evident. This was especially the case in
the marginal areas where many women farmed on their own while husbands were absent because of off-farm employment or wood cutting. For
example, Helen, who related that her husband "was never at home," did
most chores involving eight sows and getting the weanlings to market.
Ruth, also from the southern slopes of Riding Mountain, related that her
parents did not usually sell any livestock but, when taxes had to be paid or
some other expense became pressing, a cow or another farm animal was
sold. Since her mother looked after the livestock both in the summer, when
her father worked as a thresher on southern farms, and in the winter, when
he was cutting wood in the bush, the marketing of farm animals to meet
immediate cash needs was really her mother's contribution to farm fi-
nances. Similarly, Henry, whose parents farmed on poor land near Notre
Dame de Lourdes, related that, in order to pay the threshing bill each year,
they sold what they could, "like cows and grain and . . . cordwood." Henry's
mother had about ten milk cows, which she looked after by herself. The
sale of one or more of her cows was a crucial cash contribution to the
operating costs of the farm. Many farm women probably also sold milk for
income. Most local histories note the existence of a cheese factory in town
during the early years of settlement, which suggests that milk was bought
from surrounding farms. For example, the local history of Rapid City reports, "The first industry in the Moline district was 'The Hampton Cheese
Factory' established in 1891. . . . The factory was centrally located. As the
settlers moved in and started farming one of their necessities was to own
one or more cows. The farmers delivered their excess milk to the factory

and received credit and payment at regular intervals. Cheese was a very important part of their diet so when required a family would take home 'a cheese.' . . . The cost of the cheese would be deducted from that family's credit for milk."[52] While farm women marketed a great variety of farm products, eggs, poultry, and garden produce were, no doubt, the most common products bartered or sold. As noted, this income-generating strategy was most important in marginal areas but took on added significance in the prime agricultural areas during economic downturns.

In addition to marketing unprocessed farm products, many women boosted family income by marketing value-added products. For example, on some farms women undertook the manufacture of clothes and other articles as a cottage industry. Edith Gibson wrote in her family history that her mother made financial contributions to farm and family by making "dresses and hats for her new found friends."[53] Similarly, Ruth used to sew "for everyone in the district," and made shirts for men, which she sold for twenty-five cents each. The money went towards buying the groceries. Several farm women also made pillows, quilts, tablecloths, and the like for sale. Doris's mother, for example, sold her crocheted articles. The income was spent on household items. Many women also sold value-added products, like processed meats and vegetables, which generated higher returns than did raw foods. For example, some women bartered or sold processed pork. Mrs. Bell's account of farm life around 1880 in and near Rathwell indicates that country stores accepted salted pork in exchange for groceries.[54] Jennifer, whose parents lived in a rural town during the Depression, told me that her mother used to buy canned chicken from a farm woman. Carol told me how she and her husband "sometimes killed and cleaned a pig for private customers to make extra money." Some women were also involved in baking to generate income or, as in the case of Nellie McClung's mother, to generate a return of services in kind. She not only baked for a neighbour who reciprocated with carpentry but also manufactured medicine like balm of Gilead salve, which she sold to neighbours or bartered for services.[55] The exchange of services was common. Money was scarce, and labour, an equally indispensible resource in farming, was costly. The production of goods and services by women in return for labour services was, therefore, a significant in-kind contribution to farm development.

Two cottage industries that were common on a large scale across the province were buttermaking and, later on, the production of cream. The butter destined for market was packed in tubs and, in more recent times, in one-pound butter prints. Butter meant for home consumption or private customers was usually packed in crocks. This aspect of buttermaking is described in great detail by pioneer woman Emma Carlson, in an article entitled "Pioneer Women and Butter" published in the local history of Erickson.

> Butter for market was packed in wooden tubs that could be had in various sizes. These were usually well soaked in water to "draw" out any taste of wood, but, in spite of that, the butter could take on the flavour if stored in them for any length of time. . . . [With] the one-pound wooden butter print and waxed butter paper now available, . . . butter tubs had had their day. . . . Clay crocks were also available. They were ideal for packing butter, both for home use and private customers. Many a five- or ten-pound crock of butter found its way directly from the farm to the town kitchen. If butter was well washed and worked free of buttermilk and evenly salted, packed in a crock and covered with a layer of salt or an inch of strong brine, the summer's bounty could be well preserved for the bleaker days of fall and winter. The storekeepers welcomed the printed butter. They soon learned where the best butter came from and were known to set it aside for their own use and for favoured customers. The ladies producing it were the uncrowned dairy queens of their day.[56]

Butter was probably the most important farm product bartered and sold by farm women in the pioneer period. One historical source noted, "In addition to supplying their own table requirements, it was a well established custom with many settlers or, more specifically, the settlers' wives to milk a few cows and to make butter in amounts sufficient to trade or pay (in whole or in part) for family purchases at the local store."[57] This source notes further, "Where a surplus of cream over family requirements was produced, such surplus in the earlier years was used to produce homemade butter for barter at country stores or, in later years, to be shipped as cream to creameries—a practice on which many farm women depended for cash income."[58] The local history of Rathwell also suggests that women's production and marketing of butter was important in the early days of settlement. "In the years just after 1900, there was no shipping of cream in those days, as there were no creameries in the small towns. Most of the farm ladies made butter and packed it in crocks or butter tubs and traded it in to the local storekeeper for supplies."[59] In many instances, the returns on butter—often marketed together with eggs—were essential in making ends meet on the farm. This is illustrated by the experiences of Mr. and Mrs. St. John, who arrived on a Saskatchewan homestead in April 1902, with little money—only $2.35—and very few belongings. They were in need of building, farming, and household supplies, yet income from the sale of grain was not forthcoming within the first year. Considering their overall economic situation, Mrs. St. John's seemingly minor commercial activities in producing butter and eggs take on major economic significance. Note, for example, the following entries in her diary:

1902

April 16 . . . I churn two lbs. of butter, gather two eggs . . .

April 29 . . . churn two lbs. of butter, gather eight eggs—our income is improving.

May 19 . . . Men get home [from shopping] 7:30 p.m. They sold my eggs for 80 cents, and brought me a butter bowl for 50 cents and 25 cents' worth of muslin.

June 17 First chickens hatched—hen was set May 27.

1903

January 2 Wash, and churn six lbs. of butter. Hens are laying two eggs a day.

January 12 Nice winter day. Seward and Otto go to Milestone for groceries. I send 10 lbs. of butter to trade for our needs.

February 11 . . . I churn four lbs. butter and iron.

March 30 . . . churn three lbs. butter, gather 14 eggs.[60]

It is evident from Mrs. St. John's diary notations that her income-generating activities gradually expanded as circumstances allowed. Moreover, her diary leaves no doubt that her income from butter and eggs was crucial in paying for household supplies and family needs. Examples from Manitoba illustrate a similar economic dependence on the sale of butter and eggs. Rathwell farm woman Donna told me during our interview that in "the old days" she and her mother made butter from the milk of twelve cows. She explained that the income derived from selling this butter, plus whatever eggs the family could spare, was the farm's mainstay in the 1920s and 1930s, when her parents were experiencing "bad times." Her father made so little money on grain that there "wasn't even enough money to pay his taxes." In fact, she said, most of the time there was not enough grain to sell at all. It is in light of these circumstances that her mother's dairying activities need to be seen. Indeed, Donna asserted, "That's what we lived on; we made butter and sold the butter and eggs to buy the groceries." Annie, whose parents also farmed near Rathwell, had similar recollections of that time. She, too, asserted, "We really depended on the products we could sell like butter, eggs and cream." Most people I interviewed on this issue indicated that the returns on women's farm products like butter and eggs paid for the groceries. However, while this was perhaps the most common allocation of farm women's cash incomes, some women are known to have produced far more than was necessary for the purchase of family provisions. For example, one farm woman noted how she produced 100 pounds of butter per week for market.[61] The income from this amount of butter was far in excess of weekly costs of purchased family provisions. Such large-scale marketing activities probably took place most successfully in rural districts located near developing urban centres, like Winnipeg, Brandon, Rapid City, and Minnedosa. Growing towns and cities served as a large market for agricultural products. Farm women living close to these markets could expand their production processes into relatively large-scale operations. This is illustrated by Jodie's grandmother, who ran a profitable butter and egg business near Winnipeg. Jodie related:

> My grandparents came to Manitoba from eastern Canada in the 1880s. Grandmother ran the entire business [on the new farmstead]. Grandfather only worked in the field. Grandmother milked, creamed and made butter. She also redid bad butter from [neighbouring] women which she bought cheaply. She then hauled it into Winnipeg with the teamster. Eggs too. She also bought up eggs in the neighbourhood and then sold them in Winnipeg. She made enough money to buy a half section [320 acres] of land and expand [the farm]. She also paid for new equipment and so on. Grandmother was a great business woman. She never slaved in the fields but financed the whole business with her butter and eggs; her own marketing.

As this example shows, women realized the economic potential of their products and went ahead to invest their earnings directly into the cash-crop component of farm production. In fact, Jodie added that "a lot of women financed mechanization back then, all from their butter and cream and so on."

Gradually farm women shifted the marketing of dairy products from butter to cream. A number of factors played a role in this development. Government policy was intent on transforming the pattern of small-scale, local marketing of butter to a large-scale, extra-domestic, and highly profitable business. Manitoba's Department of Agriculture began promoting the production of butter in creameries rather than on farms by providing loans and training programs for creamery operators. To encourage farmsteaders to sell their cream to the creameries rather than transforming it into butter for market themselves, pick-up services were initially arranged by creameries to ease the burden of delivering cream. However, as Emma Carlson pointed out, few women needed to be convinced to sell cream instead of butter. "To work a large churning and make it into prints could be quite a heavy job. So, when another step in progress brought the creamery into the district, no one regretted leaving these chores behind for the convenience of selling cream. . . . The cream can was a welcome source of cash instead of trade, and greater emphasis was placed on year-round production. Churning on the farm was just for home use or some private customers, but even that dwindled. Creamery butter took over."[62]

Two incentives to market cream rather than butter come to light here. First of all, buttermaking became quite demanding as the amounts of butter increased. Emma Carlson elaborated: "The butterprint [or mould] made one pound of butter and then you wrapped them [the butter blocks] in wax paper later. Well, if you had, say, ten pounds you stood there pressing [the butter into the mould] and the butter had to be reasonably hard to hold its shape nicely. You would ache in your back from standing up." Not surprisingly, women gladly surrendered buttermaking in favour of selling cream. Second, as the cash economy encroached, money was becoming the only accepted means through which purchases of capital assets and other necessary items could be made. Cream generated cash. Moreover, since cream production was less labour-intensive than butter production, the time and labour saved could be invested in producing larger quantities of cream for sale. This provided farm women with the opportunity to earn far more cash than had previously been possible.

Increased production was facilitated by the introduction of the cream separator around the turn of the century. The separator permitted immediate processing of milk into cream. Previously, one had to place the milk in shallow pans in the milk house or in special cans with removeable bottoms that were hung down the well. The milk was then left for about two days for the cream to surface for skimming. This method of separating the cream limited the amount of cream that could be produced on a daily basis. So, despite the high investment cost, many farmsteaders obtained a cream separator. The local history of Rathwell recorded, for example, that the first cream separator in the district, purchased in the first decade of this century, cost eighty dollars.[63] Clearly, for that price, the purchase of a cream separator had to be worth the investment, which suggests that dairying was quite lucrative.

Just how crucial women's cream production was as an income-generating activity is illustrated by Annie, who commented, "I remember one year, we lived around Treherne and we sold cream to the creamery. I had a can that was two-thirds full of cream and I hung it down the well. That night we got rain. The next day we were supposed to take it into town. When we went down to the well in the morning the can of cream was full of water. That was the end of the cream and the groceries for that week."

Cream production was a particularly important buffering activity during the Depression of the 1930s. This is evident not only from the considerable increase in the overall cream production at the time but also from the fact that dairy cattle numbers increased, while beef cattle numbers declined. The number of creameries in the province increased during this time as well. Whereas in 1895 there had been only nineteen creameries in the province, after 1917 there were more than twice that many, and after 1939 there were more than three times that number. In 1939 and 1940 there were seventy-two creameries across the province.[64] Many farm women noted that their families relied on the cream cheque to carry them through hard times. Jodie asserted, for example, "The cream cheque was crucial back then [1930s]." Similarly, farm women from the historically prosperous Red River Valley area told me that, during the 1930s, "people made ends meet by making their own bread and butter and by taking cream to the creameries and eggs to the grocery stores." Local histories make references to the economic importance of cream during this period as well. For example, the local history of Rapid City reports: "It was in the 1930s that the highest production, of over nine hundred thousand pounds, was made. . . . Cream cheques were of utmost importance in those days."[65]

While the sale of cream was the mainstay on many Manitoba farms during economic depressions, in areas where difficult economic conditions were intrinsic rather than limited to periods of overall economic depression, the sale of cream was of ongoing importance to the viability of family farms. This is probably best illustrated by the fact that, in 1916, the provincial government passed the Settlers' Animal Purchase Act, commonly called the "Manitoba Cow Scheme." This legislation provided assistance in establishing dairy herds to struggling settlers "in the Interlake district and other needy areas."[66] Only married men were considered eligible under the program, which reflects the important role of women in dairying. It was hoped that, by stimulating dairying in chronically marginal areas, the high incidence of farm failure might be reduced. The government's plans bore fruit. The annual report to the minister of agriculture for 1917 recorded that the production of creamery butter underwent a general increase, most notably in the Interlake.[67] The Dairy Commissioner's annual report of 1918 mentioned a similar annual increase in creamery-butter output. Moreover, it noted a remarkable increase in the number of creameries in the Interlake from two to eighteen, in two years' time.[68] This indicates that Interlake farmsteaders had seized the economic opportunity to increase and stabilize their incomes by selling more cream. Farm failures in the area did indeed decrease in numbers. It was noted in the 1921 annual report that, "[prior] to the passing of the 'Settlers' Animal Purchase Act,' many homesteads in the territory between Lakes Winnipeg and Manitoba had been abandoned two to three times, and while still there may be occasional instances of this, they are extremely rare in comparison with the abandonments of former years."[69]

In this context, it is important to remember that in the marginal areas, women were often farming on their own, so that creaming for market was really *their* financial contribution to farm survival. For example, the family history of Nick and Jennie Serwa made numerous references to Jennie's extensive involvement in all aspects of the farm due to Nick's off-farm employment. In this light, the following excerpt describing the economic role of creaming on their farm is significant. "Throughout the years, some-times as many as forty cows were hand-milked. The cream was kept chilled in summer by putting it into glass gallon jugs, tying a thin rope to the jug, and letting it down into the water of a deep well. Twice a week, the jugs would be emptied into five-gallon cans (sometimes five cans a week) and shipped to the Winnipegosis creamery for two to five dollars a can. This was the only steady income of the farm and the family depended on this money a great deal to buy the bare necessities for the household."[70] In the case of the Zubrak family, cash flow had become a severe problem follow-ing the purchase of 240 acres of land and, again, during the Great Depres-sion. In both instances, the family's financial predicament was alleviated by Mrs. Zubrak's dairying activities. Mr. Zubrak related, "My wife had to work hard; [she] milked cows. . . . Ready cash was hard to get. I remember one year I took a load of grain to the elevator and figured that the seed and threshing cost me 8 cents a bushel, but the grain buyer only paid me 7 cents a bushel. The only salvation was that one could sell cream, and though the creamery did not pay much for a pound of butter fat, yet one received a little cash and was able to buy some groceries."[71]

During interviews with farm women from across the province, many comments were made on the economic role of dairying in marginal areas and the involvement of women therein. Jodie, noting the regional inequity in Manitoba's agriculture, said, for example, "It depends also on different areas in the province. Some areas are so much poorer than other areas. The land was worse. They didn't have as good a living. Once you get east from here [in Manitoba's southeastern corner] and a lot of the area in the Interlake, you get into stones. So, you can't grow grain and so that is a poor area. They are going to have cattle and so on. If they have them to milk, then the women had to work harder because they have to carry the milk and separate the milk. There would be a lot of women depending on that." Through her active role as a Women's Institute member and organizer, Jodie was, and still is, in frequent contact with women from marginal farms in southeastern Manitoba and the Interlake. Her observations for these regions of the province correspond with my own for marginal farms on the southern slopes of Riding Mountain and the eastern slopes of Duck Mountain. I spoke to several farm women from these districts and found that, for many of them, dairying had been either the mainstay or a major income supplement during many of their years on the farm. Olga related, for example, "When we got married, when a Ukrainian girl got married, her family, her father, always gives her a cow or two. That's how we started. He [father] gave them to me and I was milking them and we had a calf and later on we had more cattle. We sold cream for a living and I used to sell eggs. We had at one time twelve milking cows. I milked cows for thirty-nine years." Olga described how she supported her family on the money made by producing and selling cream:

> All the household was from cream. You didn't get very much for cream at that time. Now you get fifty dollars a can. But before, the most I used to get was twelve dollars a can. But that kept everything going; the cream cheque. I don't think we'd have survived, because we didn't have that much grain or that much of anything. The cream kept the flour, sugar, and the curtains and kids' books and clothes, hydro and everything going. Everything was paid out of that. And that was the whole year round. Whatever he [Olga's husband] made outside, from cattle or pigs; some of that went to the bank; some of it went for expenses. Whatever he sold, I didn't take anything of that.

Like Olga, Mary made significant financial contributions towards her family's well-being and the continuity of her father's farm after her mother passed away. She said, "I used to sell one can, a five gallon cream can a week. It was a hardship for that, because there was no way the cream truck could get into our place. So, I used to haul it to the store two miles. I hitched up a team and then took it. But it was nice [to have the money] coming. Somebody said, 'Oh, does she want to be bothered milking cows?' But, that was my income for the week! Yes, I made money by taking cream into town." After Mary got married in the late 1940s, she continued to milk cows and sell cream. This was an important source of income since she and her husband had started farming on rented land and other farm income was slow in coming. After seventeen years of diligent saving, they were able to buy their own farm. Mary told me proudly, "We didn't borrow, we had saved cash." She also noted that she and her husband bought a new tractor and a new deeptiller in the early 1950s with cash. By milking as many as fourteen cows, Mary's dairying activities helped finance the farm.

In conclusion, through careful economizing and a variety of income-generating activities, women played a major role in buffering against dropping standards of living and farm failure in marginal areas and in difficult economic times. In prosperous areas and times, women contributed to farm development both indirectly through financing family provisioning, thereby avoiding the diversion of income from grain for this purpose, and directly through investing their earnings into farm assets.

4.
Women in Farming in Recent Times

Women's Work during the Post-War Boom

After the Depression, fundamental changes in the nature of agriculture took place. First of all, the new economic stability in prairie agriculture, based on favourable commodity prices and good weather conditions, encouraged many farm families to focus their production on grain or livestock. Mixed farming gave way to highly specialized, commercial farming. Many farms ceased to produce for family subsistence. This was evident from the gradual disappearance of milk cows, pigs, and poultry from farmyards. Census data revealed that, between 1956 and 1966, an eight percent decrease occurred in the number of farms reporting cattle raising; a twenty-three percent decrease in the number of farms reporting having milk cows; a twenty-four percent decrease in the number of farms reporting having chickens; and a twelve percent decrease in the number of farms reporting raising pigs.[1]

Secondly, processes like farm mechanization and expansion, which had been retarded during the 1930s, continued after the Second World War at a rigorous pace. Tractors replaced draught horses, cars and trucks replaced horse-drawn buggies and grain wagons, swathers replaced binders, and combines replaced threshing machines. The same census data show a twenty-three percent decrease in the number of farms keeping horses. As one historical source pointed out: "In 1971, there was one car per farm, two trucks, two tractors, and nearly one combine."[2] In addition, farmers began using new equipment that automated putting up hay and straw, milking cows, feeding livestock, and removing manure. Coupled with genetic engineering and agro-chemicals, mechanization contributed immensely to greater farm productivity. But, because farmsteaders acquired this new machinery and adopted new farming methods, their cost of production increased. Between 1956 and 1976, for example, farm-operating costs rose by a factor of five.[3] This acted as an incentive to further increase productivity through farm expansion. Between 1941 and 1971, farm size in Manitoba increased from an average of 291 acres per farm to 543 acres.[4] More land meant more work and, as a result, men were drawn increasingly into the commodity-production components of their farms. This was facilitated by the nature of the new equipment. Tractors, unlike horses, did not need a rest, permitting operators to work longer hours. In addition, the elimination through mechanization of manual tasks previously performed by hired help increased the workload of farm operators, who now carried out these tasks themselves with the new equipment.

Farm expansion also resulted in fewer families farming. Between 1941 and 1971, the total number of farms in Manitoba dropped from 58,024 to 34,981,[5] causing a decline in Manitoba's rural population, a process that, in turn, affected rural community life. Initially, local industries such as gristmills, sawmills, and creameries were shut down as centralized corporations bought them out. In many towns, branch-railway lines and elevators were closed down as well. Ongoing rural depopulation reduced the client base of such local businesses as equipment dealerships and retail outlets, and affected the viability of such rural services as post offices, law offices, health-care services, schools, churches, and recreation facilities. The trend towards rural-town decline was reinforced by the increasing mobility of rural people. The completion of the provincial highway system in 1950, and the widespread availability of the car and truck, allowed rural inhabitants to frequent larger service centres. Many farm people I spoke to commented on the changing orientation of rural people from local communities to stores, dealerships, and recreational facilities in urban areas, resulting in a further decline in rural services. But as rural services closed down, more time spent in travelling became unavoidable. Grain had to be hauled over greater distances, and machinery parts and groceries could be acquired in more remote centres only where such goods were still available.

The changes that took place in agriculture and rural life had far-reaching implications for women's work on the farm. First of all, with the increasing involvement of men in commercial production, women began to absorb the tasks of taking meals, vehicles, and workers to the field as part of their farm work. Now that the automobile was available, women became the designated "go-fors" on the farm. Moreover, women began to assume responsibilty for farm errands such as going for parts, getting farm machinery, and trucking grain to the bin and elevator. With the closure of services in local communities, many farmers had to go farther to do these errands, and they became increasingly time-consuming. Secondly, as farming turned into a business involving complex management decision-making, women gradually took on administrative responsibilities such as answering business phone calls and relaying messages, preparing income-tax statements, gathering and filing information, and keeping financial and production records. Given their new role as farm "go-fors," many women also came to assume responsibilty for banking and paying bills. Surveys carried out among farm women in recent years show the extent to which women are involved in transportation services and administrative work on the farm. For example, a study done in 1986 among 120 Manitoba farm women revealed that eighty-eight percent of the respondents went for supplies and parts, seventy-seven percent kept financial records, seventy-five percent kept production records, forty-nine percent prepared budgets and tax returns, ninety-three percent paid farm bills, seventy-nine percent prepared bills and statements, seventy-seven percent collected information used in decision-making, and ninety-nine percent answered telephone calls and relayed messages.[6]

The new role of women on the farm is illustrated by the work experiences of the farm women I interviewed. For example, most took meals to the fields. Sandy explained that, whereas in the past women only prepared lunch for the field, they now had to take supper to the field as well. Although they did not have to cater to large threshing crews anymore, farm women now had to carry out the extra tasks of packing and transporting suppers. Cheryl noted, for example, that "it is so much easier to put it on the table than to pack everything." In recent years, some women have stopped taking supper to the fields but they still drive to the fields to pick up the men. This is time-consuming, as Brenda noted. "I couldn't put hours on it. Between running around and making meals and chasing the men off the field [to eat], it really varies from day to day. They [the men] are combining with two combines and one is at one end of the field so you have to tell him when the supper is ready. And the other one is at the other end, so you have to go tell that one. I find that a lot of time is wasted, a lot of my time. I find that I am not doing work and yet I am chasing around for them." Brenda mentioned that she still takes meals out to the field when her husband and his partner are pressed for time during harvest.[7]

Most farm women I talked to also go for repairs and haul grain. Many haul chemicals and livestock and move vehicles on the farm as well. For example, Nicole mentioned, "In the springtime, I haul fertilizer and do the running back and forth [from field to house] and the running for repairs."

She added that she also hauls grain and hogs. Susan described her involvement in similar work. "Do you ever watch baseball? You know, they have a designated hitter. I decided I was the designated 'go-for.' Go for parts and repairs to the combine; sometimes hauling grain." The farm women I interviewed are generally all involved in administrative work as well. Linda, for example, answers business calls, relays messages, and handles the mail on her farm. Irene does all the banking and bill paying. She became the farm's secretary-treasurer after it was incorporated. Similarly, Wilma does the banking and bill paying on her family's incorporated farm, and combines this with bookkeeping. She told me that she spends one day per week on updating records. Another farm woman, Carol, described her work in a similar fashion: "I look after the cheques, go to the bank, look after the telephone bills and hydro bills and do the shopping. I haul the grain into town with a half-ton truck and when the elevator agent writes out the grain cheque, I take it to the Credit Union and deposit it in our bank account. I also do most of the correspondence and phoning, like to banks and the like." By incorporating transportation services and administrative tasks into their work schedules, women contribute to the commercial production process on the farm by freeing men from these detailed and time-consuming chores. This was particularly evident from Barbara's account. She noted how, in this day and age, "there is more things to know as a farm manager.... Farm women," she said,

> collect all the literature on chemicals and file it and they clip the newspapers and the articles and so when the guys sit down and read, it is really productive reading time. I do this for my husband, I will circle the paper. Like, the papers are piled up here for three weeks and some days I'll sit down and I'll circle them all and mark a lot of stuff. Then he reads it. I circle articles on the economy and chemicals or a new development or a new piece of equipment or something like that. Lots of gals do that, just to try to make the time [for husbands] as productive as we can because they [husbands] are overloaded all the time, at least my husband is, and I think most of them are.

Another farm woman, Irene, also described the time- and energy-consuming aspects of bookkeeping. She remarked that if her husband had had to assume the administrative role, this would have compromised the commercial production process on their farm, a large, incorporated business. She said:

> I have kept the books from the beginning. Taking the deposits to the bank, that's how it all started! I have kept at least half a dozen different

bookkeeping systems, to try them out. Nowadays, I keep a "loose ledger," feeding all information into the computer. I cried a lot when I was learning to use the computer. I didn't have much help really. I drove into Winnipeg. They have an education centre there and I took a day on each of a couple of things. And, when I came home I bugged some of my friends over the phone. But, mostly, I learned out of the manual. I take a couple of hours a week [to update the books] and, then, longer on the month's end because I do profit and loss; a complete print out.

After the war, women's work in farm administration and transportation did not often go hand in hand with involvement in other aspects of commodity production on the farm. With the exception of hauling grain and sometimes livestock, women on prosperous farms continued to spend little time on field tasks. Mechanized equipment enabled their husbands to carry out most fieldwork by themselves, while better returns on farm commodities after the Depression made hired help financially affordable. Laura noted that "in the spring, the field only needs to be cultivated, harrowed and seeded, and one person can do that," while Barbara, Irene, and Norah mentioned the presence of hired help in their fields. As with field tasks, the mechanization of tasks related to commercial livestock raising displaced women from this production sphere on many specialized livestock farms. Shirley, for example, noted the use of a new haybaler and a tractor with a front-end loader as a factor in her withdrawal from haying and feeding chores. Similarly, Brenda mentioned the mechanization of milking in her family's dairy operation as a reason she no longer milks. In other words, while women came to provide essential services related to commodity production after the war, they tended not to share in the direct, hands-on farm work. Mechanization was a major factor contributing to this division of labour.

Perhaps more important were the changes in the technological system related to housework that continued to draw women away from commodity production into domestic work. In 1946, the Manitoba Power Commission undertook a program of rural electrification, which, for homes in rural towns, was completed in 1954. But many farm homes did not receive electricity until the 1960s. Electricity in rural homes changed the scope of domestic work. Electric household appliances eliminated the tedium of many tasks. For example, with electric cookstoves, the need for wood cutting and hauling disappeared. Automatic food processors, blenders, and dough mixers reduced the work of cutting, beating, and mixing food. However, the actual cooking tasks remained the same. Therefore, while the assistance of men, children, and servants in supplying fuel became obsolete and their participation in processing food was reduced, women's share of the workload in food preparation did not diminish. In fact, the operation and maintenance of these sophisticated appliances were added to their domestic workload. Similarly, for housecleaning, it was generally women who operated new equipment such as electric vacuum cleaners and floor polishers. The amount of help women received from children and servants who had once been involved in beating and sweeping rugs and scrubbing floors was considerably less. When higher prosperity levels after the Depression allowed farm families to have bigger homes and more furniture, women's workload in housecleaning increased dramatically. The introduction of running water in the home had a similar effect on the nature of domestic work. Although tedious tasks like carrying water to and from the house were eliminated, new ones emerged. For example, with indoor plumbing there were now the new tasks of cleaning toilets, bathtubs, sinks, and water taps. Moreover, running water in the home enabled people to adopt higher standards of cleanliness, which meant that bathrooms, kitchens, and clothing were cleaned more frequently than had been done in the past.

While the availability of electricity and running water in the home was an important factor in altering women's work in the home, three additional factors reinforced this development. First of all, men were drawn away from domestic production by the expansion of commercial production on the farm. Secondly, obligatory school attendance legislated in the first half of this century pulled children out of domestic tasks. And, finally, rural depopulation eroded the base from which domestic help could be hired. Various surveys have shown the high proportion of housework done by women alone. For example, a national survey done in 1982 by the National Farmers' Union shows that nearly eighty-six percent of household tasks were done by women, with husbands contributing only seven percent and other household members making up the difference.[8] Another national study shows that thirty-three percent of husbands did not do any domestic work at all; and that, for those who did assist, it was most likely with financial management and child care. Husbands were least likely to assist with looking after the family's clothing, food preparation, care of the sick, and housecleaning.[9] A provincial study done among Manitoba women in 1986 shows that they performed seventy-nine percent of the domestic work. Husbands did less than ten percent while other household members did seventeen percent.[10] These provincial figures, like the national ones, support the argument that women are the main workers in the domestic sphere on the farm.

The advent of the automobile contributed to further changes in women's domestic work. Women replaced men as suppliers of essential household products and, as farm families consumed more and more industrial products, this work became increasingly demanding. Greater cash flow on Manitoba farmsteads meant that farm families began to purchase goods and services in the store, which had formerly been produced on the farm, such as meat, eggs, milk, fruit, soap, pharmaceutical items, and clothing. Women came to make regular trips to supermarkets, pharmacies, and clothing stores in nearby service centres. Therefore, although the decline in home production of family products reduced the labour of women in related tasks, it did not yield a net saving of time in family provisioning. Ruth Cowan, the author of a book on the history of housework in North America, noted in this respect: "By mid century the time that housewives had once spent in preserving strawberries and stitching petticoats was being spent in driving to stores, shopping, and waiting in lines."[11] The automobile contributed to another development in women's domestic work; that is, the creation of "a host of other transportation services (such as taking children to parties and to doctors) that women of an earlier generation had not provided for their families."[12]

This development coincided with a change in social values about child rearing, whereby emphasis was placed on the personal development of children through extracurricular activities. Mothers began to transport children to music lessons, ballet, hockey practice, figure skating, and so on. In addition, they were expected to participate in children's pursuits through personal guidance. This augmented women's work in child rearing, as can be observed from weekly schedules of farm women with young children. For example, Georgina drives her son to piano lessons and hockey practice every Monday, spending four hours in the process. On Wednesdays, Fridays, and Saturdays, she drives her daughter to figure skating, ballet, and gymnastics, taking about an hour and a half each day. In addition to these activities, Georgina spends one hour every evening helping her son with piano practice. Similarly, Linda spends several hours per week taking her children to skating and piano lessons and gymnastics. In addition, she spends the evenings helping her daughter with piano practice, helping with the children's homework, and reading stories before they go to bed. As recreational facilities close down in local communities, women find themselves spending more and more time on the road, transporting children to centres where facilities are still available, a situation becoming increasingly common in rural areas. For example, Cathy, who for several years drove her children to Hamiota for piano lessons, a thirty-two-mile round trip, taking one hour in driving alone, had to take them to another piano teacher in Kenton, an eighty-mile round trip, taking an hour and a half. Moreover, she drove one of her children to Brandon for special voice lessons, a round trip of 150 miles, taking three hours. In other words, despite the fact that families were getting smaller, child rearing became more demanding. While children were, at one time, *producers* in the farm household, helping their mothers with gardening, cooking, cleaning, and babysitting, they increasingly became *consumers* of goods and services produced by their mothers.

Child care has become demanding in yet another way. Mothers are expected by the community to participate in organizations to which their children belong. For example, Liz related, "I find that the things the children are in, I have to be in too. It's a small community and as a mother you have to show your interest, especially with four kids. You can't just dump them and go your own merry way." As a result, Liz teaches Sunday School, coordinates figure skating, and is a 4-H leader. Similarly, Wilma, who donates labour and food to the local Scout and skating clubs, and is the secretary treasurer of the Cub Scouts, commented, "I have had this brought up to me several times. For example, [during fund-raising events] you donate the food and pies and all that. Everybody in the community is expected to do this." As rural communities lose inhabitants and services, the struggle to keep recreational facilities open places extra demands on women's time and labour. Cathy noted this can become a burden when the population base from which to draw women's volunteer support diminishes:

> The rink is a focal point in a lot of communities and they [people in communities] want artificial ice and all these great things. But, the community has to be able to afford it. So, one of the ways that you can afford it, in my community, is you provide lunches every night of the week, seven days a week, from October to April. You are supposed to take your turn and, for the most part, it is women that do this. We want to have a rink so that our children can play hockey and do figure skating, and so we can curl and all that. But it becomes a great burden, a *great* burden!

In conclusion, despite the mechanization of housekeeping and the availability of processed foods, manufactured clothes, and professional health care, women's workload in the domestic sphere was not reduced. This conclusion finds support in national and provincial surveys. For example, a survey of Manitoba farm women found that respondents spent fifty-four hours per week in family and household work.[13] This figure coincides with the findings of national surveys, one of which concluded on the basis of its research that with the "proliferation of time-saving appliances to ease the household work-load, one would think that the 52 hours spent by the average farmwife in 1924 (U.S.A.) would be greatly reduced, yet research studies show that almost no change had occurred in the last 50 years."[14]

This study also reported a significant difference in the weekly number of hours spent in housework by women with and women without children; that is, nearly fifty-nine hours compared to just over forty hours, respectively.[15] This indicates the labour-intensive nature of child rearing.

In the decades after the war, when agriculture underwent a general upswing and prosperity levels increased, farm women relaxed their economizing and income-generating activities. Moreover, with women becoming increasingly responsible for child rearing and household work, many had to adjust these economic activities to accommodate their busy schedules. Subsistence production on the farm decreased. Nancy commented, for example, that she cut back on gardening "to spend as much time as possible with the children." Another farm woman, Wilma, related, "We spend about thirteen hundred dollars per year on milk because we are with the six of us. That would very nicely pay for a cow, but who is going to milk it? That is the problem. I already do everything else around here. There are times that you have to draw a line as to what you are going to do."

In addition to women's busy schedules, other factors played a role in the decline of home provisioning on the farm. Higher levels of farm prosperity, which permitted the purchase of consumer goods, was one. The year-round availability of fresh fruit, vegetables, meat, and eggs at relatively low prices was another. Yet another was easier access to stores, thanks to all-season roads and rapid transportation. And, finally, the appeal of advertising, especially to rural youths, changed tastes and desires. Several farm women noted the effect of these factors on their home-provisioning activities. Carol commented, for example, "I used to do a lot of sewing for the kids, until the youngest was about eight. Then I quit because now kids want designer jeans and camouflage vests." Another farm woman, Barbara, said, "We have a grain farm and a feedlot. When we ship beef, I don't even keep a half. I buy it off the meat counter because it is cheaper and we can buy the cuts that we want. We used to raise a steer for beef. Now I just go to the store, the same as the gal in the city." Wilma, too, mentioned the availability of relatively cheap poultry products in the store as a reason for not raising chickens and said, "I don't have chickens because the time and work involved in keeping chickens simply does not pay for itself." Another woman commented, "There was more money around [and] farm families started buying more in stores. In the late 1970s, everybody started to buy cottage cheese, cheese and eggs. Farmers milk less now. Some even quit completely. They couldn't be bothered anymore. Milk and cheese are available through the store. So they started to do less [home production] because it is too much work to milk and make cottage cheese and butter and so on."

Not all farm women substituted industrial products for homemade ones at the same rate and to the same extent. A provincial survey carried out among 120 Manitoba farm women in 1986 shows the extent to which women have relinquished the home production of vegetables and preserves. Eighty-three percent of the respondents kept vegetable gardens on a regular basis; fifteen percent on an occasional basis; and two percent kept no garden at all. Eighty-eight percent of the respondents preserved food for family consumption on a regular basis; eleven percent did so occasionally; and one percent did not do so at all.[16] These statistics reflect my own observations for Manitoba farm women. For example, although many of the farm women I interviewed had stopped producing beef, pork, poultry, and dairy products for family consumption, nearly all had continued keeping gardens, preserving vegetables and fruit, and baking bread and pastries. However, the extent to which they carried out these activities varied between providing food to meet almost all family needs to providing merely a fraction. Many supplemented home-produced pastries, garden produce, and preserves with store-bought goods. Similarly, most women combined home manufacture of clothes with purchasing. My observations with respect to the production of livestock products for family provisioning find support in a national survey of 1982: only thirty-two percent of the farm women surveyed cared for animals used for family consumption on a regular basis; thirty-four percent did so occasionally; and thirty-four percent did not do so at all.[17] With respect to making clothes, another national study, carried out in 1979, shows that only about sixty percent of its 908 respondents manufactured family clothing.[18] Although this figure implies that this activity continues to be carried out on a sizeable scale, it also shows that many women have relinquished it. The study also found that sixty-six percent of its Manitoba respondents reported doing less work in the 1970s in home production than before.[19]

Home production as an income-generating activity of farm women appears to have decreased in the decades after the war as well. One of the reasons may be the availability of factory-made products, which replaced traditional, homemade ones. Another reason is greater farm prosperity, which reduced the need for extra farm income. Shrinking local markets, related to the ongoing processes of rural depopulation and rural-town decline, also played a role. And an additional factor may be industry and government regulations on sanitation and productivity. Uninspected meat, eggs, and dairy products could no longer be sold through retail stores. Several farm women commented on the effect of some of these factors on the production of goods on the farm for sale. Helen noted, for example, that "times got better and many farmers quit milking because they didn't need that money anymore." At the same time, however, women engaged in other income-generating activities, like off-farm employment, on a limited scale. After the war, a number of farm women continued to contribute to the expansion and mechanization of their farms in this way. Natalie, who worked in a printing office and drove a school bus for several years after her marriage in the early 1960s, explained, for example, how she allocated her income from these jobs. "I didn't save it, although I have my own bank account. But, that's the way we [my husband and I] did it. Anything we earned, it all pretty well went into the farm; into building up the farm so that we didn't have to borrow any money." Similarly, Norah related how she contributed to the development of her and her husband's farm through income earned as a nurse. Starting with 160 acres of land and only some basic equipment, Norah's income from nursing enabled them to gradually expand and mechanize. "The money I earned we lived on. The money or whatever my husband made went back into the farm, because that is what we wanted to do; trying to make a good farm. We expanded the farm as we went along and when we could afford it." These examples illustrate that women who worked off the farm contributed to the development of the farm in both direct ways, through investment in farm assets, and indirect ways, by contributing financially to the household budget.

Effects of the Farm Crisis

The overall upswing in agriculture after the Second World War came to an abrupt end in the late 1970s. By the early 1980s, interest rates and the cost of production had climbed to record highs and farm-commodity prices began to drop to record lows. Concurrently, farm incomes dropped and a great many Canadian farm families experienced financial distress, suffering from severe cash-flow problems. The crisis conditions are shown in statistics published later in the 1980s. For example, Farm Credit Corporation figures of 1987 show that eight percent of Canada's farm operators were insolvent and that another twenty-three percent had cash-flow problems, leading to insolvency.[20] Almost one-third of Canadian farm operators were on the verge of going broke. Many already had. Between 1979 and 1987, a total of 3356 farm families went bankrupt in Canada, of which 349 were in Manitoba.[21] These figures tell only part of the story. They do not include farm families who left the farm after selling out quietly or through foreclosure. The 1986 Census of Agriculture shows that 2106 Manitoba families had left the farm between 1981 and 1986 alone, a 7.2 percent decline, leaving merely 27,336 families on the farm in 1986.[22] As farm families leave the land, farm-service industries close down as well, adding to the problem of rural-town decline. This situation is not likely to change. Farm families face further declines in real, net farm income. Agriculture Canada predicted that farm incomes in 1990, after expenses, might fall by eighty-seven percent in Manitoba. In the last seven months of 1989, the number of Manitoba farm families facing foreclosure jumped forty-six percent, compared with the same period in 1988.[23]

Since the 1980s, dwindling farm incomes have caused women to in-crease, once again, their direct involvement in commodity production on the farm through participation in fieldwork and livestock keeping. First of all, low farm incomes have meant that many husbands have sought off-farm employment, and, secondly, hired help has become less affordable. As a result, women have taken up the slack by doing farm chores. According to Maureen, a farm woman from south-central Manitoba, it is now quite common to see women working in the fields. She explained, "In our area there were a lot of specialized [grain] farms that were well off. Therefore, the women didn't go out and do things in the field. *Now* it seems they do more fieldwork than when I was young, because now, if they [their hus-bands] have combines and trucks which are all easy to run, the women drive the truck or do whatever. Then they [their husbands] don't need to hire a man at all. That just wipes out paying wages. Therefore, the women are working harder, or, at least, they are taking more of an active role." As in previous depressions, women's participation in farm-commodity produc-tion today economizes on labour expenses when farm income is low. In December 1984, in an article entitled "Farm Women Working Harder," the Winnipeg *Free Press* reported that women's participation in fieldwork and livestock raising is

> critical today, with growing numbers of farms in Canada in danger of failing because of high interest rates and low prices for farm produce.... The Federal Farm Credit Corporation estimates that . . . as many as 17 percent of its clients are under financial pressure. . . . That pressure has forced many farm women to roll up their sleeves even higher in order to hold onto the homestead. . . . Audrey Turbett, whose family runs a dairy farm just outside Winnipeg, says a number of livestock farms in the area have had to lay off hired hands to save money. . . . "A lot of women are helping out more in the barn," says Turbett, who adds she still heaves her share of hay bales as well as doing the bookkeeping.[24]

Apart from the fact that hired help has become less affordable, the accel-erating trend towards rural depopulation has meant that hired help, especially skilled hired help, has also become less available. As a result, women are training themselves to become experienced equipment operators and in this way buffer against labour shortages on their farms. Many have taken advantage of the courses on farm mechanics and safety offered by Assiniboine Community College for women across the province. Manitoba farm women do not stand alone in their response to the economic crisis in agriculture. Respondents to a nation-wide survey among rural women noted "the high wages and low availability of hired help" as the major incentives for their increased participation in commodity production.[25] Although these respondents also identified a number of other factors, such as smaller families and more automated domestic appliances, my research has shown that, on the whole, these changes did not provide women with more time for participation in commodity production. In fact, most farm women carry a double workload. They work in commodity production while remaining responsible for nearly all domestic work. Another national study found that women who are on the farm full-time do eighty-seven percent of the housework and eighteen percent of the farm work.[26] The following examples show the economizing and buffering role of women's participation in commodity production. They also illustrate the new division of labour between men and women in fieldwork and barn work.

In the first example we meet Wilma Jones, who, together with her husband and parents-in-law, farms several sections of land in western Manitoba. Half the farm income comes from cattle and the other half is from grain. Although Wilma and her husband own a few sections of land together, most of the farm is co-owned with her parents-in-law. Wilma and her husband are in the process of taking over the entire farm. She told me that they owe her husband's parents well over half a million dollars. Although the Jones family can be considered prosperous and well established, they have financial worries. Wilma related that, as a result of the current crisis in Canadian agriculture, their net farm income has dropped while input costs have risen. This has placed them in a precarious situation. Wilma stated that their financial position at the bank has not improved in the last five years and that their operating loans have grown. The farm employs three full-time workers, one of whom works year-round and the others on a seasonal basis. Despite the hired help, Wilma invests many hours of labour in the farm. "I fill in wherever it is needed," she said. During the calving season in the spring, Wilma participates in checking on the bred cows. During the growing season, her main job is baling hay and straw for the cattle while the men work in the grain fields. At the time of our interview, she had just finished putting up 20,000 bales of straw and, while she had

had some assistance from the men in haying, she had raked all the second-cut hay by herself. Wilma also combines occasionally in the harvest season and does most of the grain hauling. "In addition," she related, "I test the grain [for dryness] and I call at the elevator." She added that she calls "the elevator all the time to find out the prices and to ask if we can deliver the wheat." Because her husband spends a lot of time away from the farm on business, Wilma's involvement in commodity production includes giving orders to the hired men and dealing with suppliers and dealers. She also keeps the books and does all the banking. Wilma estimates that she does twenty-five percent of the fieldwork and barn work; 100 percent of the bookkeeping; ninety-five percent of all household work; and most of the farm errands and child care. She has four school-age children. Her husband contributes little to the domestic work, she said. He cooks occasionally but, as a rule, never launders, cleans, or bakes. Wilma's heavy involvement in the farm is crucial. Considering the size of the enterprise and its multifaceted production structure, Wilma and her husband increasingly need each other's help in managing the farm and sharing the workload. In addition, the current crisis in agriculture, which has caused a drop in income at a time when Wilma and her husband are paying off heavy debts, has given strong impetus to her growing farm involvement.

About 100 kilometres to the south of the Jones's farm, Diana and Clark Irving operate a grain farm. The farm, over 1000 acres in size, is in serious financial trouble. Like so many of the financially troubled farm families in Manitoba today, the Irving family expanded their operation at a time when rising interest rates and falling grain prices were just around the corner. Because of their precarious financial situation, Diana and her husband have had to find off-farm employment to subsidize the farm operation. Diana also does a lot of the fieldwork. Her husband's mother, Jane, pitches in with the fieldwork as well. Jane, a widow in her late sixties, also operates her own grain farm. She told me that she does most of the spring work and all the summer work on her son and daughter-in-law's farm. "Our land joins each other so we work the land together. The economics makes it viable that way. If we didn't work together, we would have to have two different sets of machinery, plus my son could not work off the farm because he wouldn't have anybody to work the land when he is away. So, we work the machinery together and I do most of the land work on his farm, as well as my own." On the Irving farm, work done by adult family members has taken on a division of labour whereby Clark seeds the fields and applies chemicals in the spring, and the women pick stones and cultivate the land. In the fall, Clark generally hauls grain and fixes equipment while Diana and Jane swath and combine. After the harvest, Jane usually cultivates the land. The example of the Irving family is significant in that it shows the economizing nature of women's fieldwork. Under conditions of financial stress and male off-farm employment, this labour contribution takes on a buffering quality.

The next example illustrates women's work on a dairy farm. Ellen Smith has always worked in her family's large dairy operation. The Smith family has 190 head of cattle, of which seventy are being milked. They produce around 1250 to 1300 liters of milk per day but, despite the fact that a monthly milk cheque maintains a steady cash flow on the farm, the Smith family is not financially secure. Their net farm income—after all household needs, interest payments on bank loans, farm chemicals, feed, and wages have been paid—amounts to little more than $3000 per year on average. Although the farm employs one full-time and two part-time workers on a year-round basis, and most of the labour processes—such as milking, barn and equipment cleaning, grain growing, haying, and feed mixing—have been automized, the farm is currently operating above its labour capacity.

According to daughter Tammy, this situation is characteristic of many farms that struggle with heavy debt loads and high interest payments, and that attempt to gain extra income by intensifying production through expansion. The Smith family are milking more cows than ever before, which has created extra work for everyone involved. However, the farm cannot afford to hire extra help, and family labour has therefore become crucial. Ellen and Tammy participate in many of the farm functions. Both do a lot of haying, and Tammy related that she is "the farm's main baler." They do feeding chores as well, which are carried out several times a day. Although feed mixing is mechanized, getting the feed to the cattle is not. Mother and daughter are therefore involved in carrying the pails of feed and bales of hay to the cows in the barn. Ellen feeds the calves after milking, which is quite labour-intensive since calves are fed milk by bottle. Ellen has always participated in milking, which involves getting the cows inside from an outside shed, placing the milking equipment on each cow for five to ten minutes, and disinfecting the udders. Ellen has also always been responsible for cleaning and sanitizing the milking equipment and milk tank, which involves both an internal and an external cleaning. The internal cleaning takes about forty-five minutes to one hour and is done twice a day, after each milking shift. I was told that cleaning involves "running hot water through the system, at the right temperature for a proper cleaning." This is followed by "running certain chemicals through the system," after which "water is run through the system once again" and then "drained in separate sinks." The internal cleaning is fully automized and Ellen basically operates the taps, which need to be turned on and off at the right time. The external cleaning takes about forty-five minutes but, according to the Smith women, "if one had the time to do it properly, following the rules, it would take up to two hours." It is carried out once a day, usually in the morning after milking. Ellen does the internal and external cleaning simultaneously, which takes an hour and a half. In addition, she cleans the milk tank every second day, after it is emptied by the milk haulers. Nowadays, this process is automized and does not take more than ten to fifteen minutes. In the past, however, it was done manually, taking twenty to sixty minutes, depending on how thoroughly the tank was cleaned.

Besides working with the dairy cattle and equipment in the barn, and haying in the fields, the Smith women also do the bookkeeping and bill paying, which, in the past, was done by Ellen alone. Although Ellen and Tammy get a wage for their work on the farm, when all hours of labour are considered, the salary amounts to little more than one dollar per hour. According to Tammy, the farm simply cannot afford to pay more, yet it desperately needs the extra labour input. This, once again, demonstrates the buffering nature of women's participation in commodity production.

On a hog farm east of Winnipeg, Joyce and her husband raise 600 hogs per year. Joyce has always been a full participant in all aspects of the operation. She looks after the fifty breeding sows when they have offspring, castrates the male piglets, and feeds and vaccinates all the hogs on the farm. Joyce told me that her heavy involvement in the hog operation was necessitated by the lack of funds to hire help.

Joyce's involvement is similar to that of Tina, who, together with her husband, operates a mixed farm west of Duck Mountain. They raise 700 hogs a year and have a beef cattle herd of approximately ninety head. The farm cannot afford to hire help. As a result, Tina works extensively with the livestock besides working full-time off the farm as a bank clerk to support the financially troubled family farm. She assists cows and sows delivering their offspring, does all the vaccinating of the livestock, and treats the animals against worms. She cuts the hogs' tails, castrates male piglets, and helps dehorn the cattle. Tina told me she does "all the doctoring" on the farm. In addition, she participates in loading animals on the truck for transport off the farm.

Marianne of Neepawa shares the operation of her family's cow/calf and feedlot operation. She assists her husband in dehorning and loading cattle, including chasing the animals into a chute. The farm has 100 head of cattle, and Marianne is generally responsible for vaccinating them and administering worm treatments. She told me that the farm does not employ any hired help and that she fills in where and whenever needed.

This is the same for Natalie, who participates heavily in her family's sheep/grain operation. At one time, the farm raised cattle and hogs as well. Natalie told me that she has always done a lot of the work with the livestock. This, she said, was necessary because her husband has always been employed off the farm and the farm has never been able to afford hired help. She said, "I do most of the farm work. You can't both be away, especially with lambing. I look after the sheep, especially during lambing time. But, also, I do the chores, like feed whatever animals we have and water them." Natalie elaborated on her involvement in sheep raising, the farm's main sphere of production. "In the winter it takes maybe half an hour a day for feeding and watering. In lambing time—that goes on for about two months—it is quite a bit more time, because you're out! At least every couple of hours you go out and check the pregnant ewes. If a lamb is born, then there are things to do. You eartag them and put them in the pen and do this and that. It takes quite a bit of time." In addition to this, Natalie assists the sheep that have trouble lambing. She mows hay and does all the baling on the farm, and she hauls and augers grain. She also participates in the administrative functions of the farm. Although her husband keeps the farm books and they each do their own banking, Natalie does all the income tax. She also does most of the farm errands such as going for repairs and supplies.

Denise, who operates a poultry farm in south-central Manitoba, is the final example of women's participation in farm-commodity production. Denise began her poultry operation in the late 1960s when prices for grain were depressed and the family's grain farm was in serious trouble. In an effort to raise extra income, Denise traded oats with another farm family for 1000 chicks. She repeated this exchange three times within the next few months and in this way started her first year as a poultry farmer with 4000 chicks. Denise manages and operates the poultry farm by herself, receiving help from her husband and children only with the more labour-intensive activities such as preparing birds for market. She earns a steady income from her poultry operation, which, she told me, helps to diversify her family's income. Denise also works alongside her husband on the family farm, participating in combining, grain hauling, and deeptilling.

These examples illustrate women's increased participation in commodity production. At the same time, they show that women's participation in transportation services and administrative work has remained high. Although task sharing between husbands and wives in farm work has increased, domestic work remains primarily women's responsibility. Some husbands help out with cooking and child care but task sharing in other aspects of housework is minimal. Yet housework has increased in scope as women attempt to save money through renewed economizing efforts.

Many farm families, particularily those that are hard hit by the economic crisis, have had to "tighten their belts" in the last several years. Since women have traditionally played a major role in "controlling family expenditures and family consumption wants," they are often the first ones to take economizing measures in the farm household.[27] Shirley illustrated this with the following comment: "My mother-in-law worked really hard and knew the ins and outs of the farm. When she passed away in the mid-1980s, my father-in-law couldn't even turn around. He didn't realize so many things, like how much it costs for hydro and telephone and how well she budgeted on buying food and clothes and how much these things cost. Men often don't realize just how good a job these women are doing—just keeping the family going on so little—and not actually realizing how little of their money goes into the household as opposed to the farm." Shirley also described how the severe cash-flow problems on her and her husband's farm affect her own financial management of the household, "even down to buying groceries. Things have been skimpy around here. You have to count your pennies every day. But it's really your lifestyle that is affected the most. You go shopping and you know you only have ten dollars to spend and you buy what you need most. There is never anything left over for anything extra, like to ever take a holiday or even buy a new pair of jeans. Sometimes [my husband] will say, when we are going somewhere, 'Why don't you have something to wear?' and I'll say, 'Well, there isn't the money; I needed milk or something else worse.'"

Similarly, Cheryl, whose family was about to lose the farm through foreclosure at the time of the interview, told how she economizes on family expenses for food. She grows a large garden and bakes bread and sweets for her family of nine. "Despite our financial trouble, we have always eaten well as far as wholesome food goes. I don't buy tinned, prepared things [processed food]. We fix it from scratch. For instance, I don't buy cookies as a rule. Once in a while, I may do that but *never* frozen pies or cakes or anything like that. Like, if I don't bake it we simply don't have it. It's not a necessity anyhow to have baked goods, although it is nice." Cheryl explained how economizing on housing expenditures has saved income for investment in the farm operation. "When we moved into this house we had the intention of building on and fixing it up and insulating it and all this. And now, all the money was always put in the farm, nothing went into the house."

The lengths to which some families must go to economize on farm and family expenses is not common to all farm families. Many still have adequate income to meet production costs and family expenses. Among other advantages, they are likely to have expanded their farm operations at opportune times; that is, before the downturn in commodity prices and higher costs of production impaired their ability to reduce their burden of loans. The women on these farms tend to be less concerned with frugality than those living on heavily indebted farms. Despite obvious attempts to economize on family expenses, financially strapped farm women today seem to have more difficulty making ends meet than in previous depressions. Relative prosperity in recent decades has allowed many to relinquish family-provisioning activities in favour of the purchase of consumer goods. This loss in self-sufficiency has meant that some farm families are now unable to meet basic food needs. I was told by Karen that "many farmers don't grow their own gardens anymore. They are not feeding themselves anymore. So, we have farmers in Canada who, once they run out of cash flow, cannot afford to put food on their family's table when they are sitting on two or three sections of land." The difficulty of making ends meet in the home is shown in a 1985 newspaper article about financial problems on prairie farms. Paraphrasing Saskatchewan farm activist Jean Argue, the reporter wrote, "She believes hundreds of farm families are on the brink of poverty. . . . Argue said she was shocked to find families going without proper food and clothing. . . . She also found a generation of farm families who are as dependent on the grocery store and packaged foods as their city counterparts. They don't raise chickens, they don't bake bread, and the grasshoppers ate their gardens. . . . But while they may try to hide it, a farm family's hard times are broadcast by their lack of spending."[28]

Other developments besides reduced self-sufficiency have affected the ability of farm families to cope successfully with the current crisis. For example, at one time, farm families drew mutual economic support by reciprocating services with other families. In recent decades, however, many of the traditional forms of cooperation, such as construction bees and beef rings, have been replaced by contract work for pay. Moreover, the incorporation of the cash economy in rural life has meant that farm women can no longer barter their homemade products for commercial ones at the local store. Both developments have reduced a farm family's ability to conserve income at a time when economizing is essential to financial survival. Therefore, as farm women's former in-kind contributions to meeting family consumption needs have diminished, many now supplement these with cash contributions to the household budget.

Many women have undertaken a variety of income-generating strategies. Seeking off-farm employment is one common strategy. At the 1987 Manitoba Farm Women's Conference, Nancy Painter noted in her closing address that "more farm women are pitching in with field work and taking jobs to subsidize the family farm....The regular paycheque an off-farm job yields will generate cash flow. . . ."[29] Newspaper columnist Penny Ham commented on the diversity of jobs held by a large proportion of the 500 farm women who attended the conference. She wrote: "And what a variety of women reside on Manitoba farms!—writers, magazine editors, lawyers, home economists, directors of development corporations, artists, teachers, nurses and even some bankers."[30] Based on my own research, this list can be extended to include travel agents, bank and store clerks, store owners and managers, waitresses, kitchen aids, cooks, gas-station attendants, librarians, office workers, bus drivers, driving instructors, caretakers, and paid workers on neighbouring farms. It is evident from comments made by older farm women, however, that the widespread adoption of off-farm employment by farm women is a relatively recent development. Irene, who farms south of Winnipeg, told me, for example, "When I got married in 1949 it was an unheard thing that you worked after you were married. It just didn't enter into your mind that if you were a farm wife, that you would commute to Winnipeg and work. Yet, when my son and daughter-in-law were married in 1976, [my daughter-in-law] just automatically continued to work. It was just an accepted thing." Likewise, farm women Laura of western Manitoba and Jodie of south-central Manitoba remarked that farm women's off-farm work was subject to criticism in the late 1940s and 1950s. "Nowadays," Laura said, "many farm women can have their own careers." She noted how this is reflected in the need to switch local Women's Institute meetings from afternoons to evenings to accommodate farm women who have off-farm jobs. I was told that, in the 1940s, '50s, and '60s, farms were able to generate enough income to support the family and farm operation without outside incomes. Nowadays, however, such income is vital to keeping farm and family going and, as a result, many farm women seek employment off the farm. Retired farm woman Cathy put it this way:

> When I was on the farm [1950s and 1960s] most women all around me were also [working exclusively] on farms. That was our jobs. But now, what has changed is that many of the women have jobs in town. They are coming to nurse, they are coming to teach, they are working as nurses'

aides and in restaurants. They do that because they need the money. The farm has to have the money to keep the thing going. The farm is not the viable operation anymore. That is how I read it. The money from the outside source—the money from the woman's job—keeps the family going. If she weren't bringing that income in, I don't know what would be happening to many of the farms now.

In the last decade, farm women who have an off-farm job have become more the rule and less the exception. Almost everyone I interviewed could name several neighbouring farms on which the women had off-farm jobs. Shirley, who farms with her husband in the ClanWilliam area south of Riding Mountain, told me, for example, "Well, here in the community there's just about fifty percent of the farm households, maybe, that have women working off the farm for the household. That is why my mom went to work. There was never any curtains around in this house or never anything extra until she did go to work." Sandy, who works off the farm as a kitchen assistant in a rural hospital, commented, "There are a lot of women with off-farm jobs in this area [around Rathwell, St. Claude, and Treherne]. In fact, there are a lot of them working where I am working. Off-farm jobs keep the family and house going. It pays for food and clothing for the kids." Responding to the question whether she knew farm women in her area, around Minnedosa and Neepawa, who worked off the farm, JoAnn remarked, "Oh yes. You wouldn't believe! There are women who are working now that I never dreamed would leave the farm. That is economics, you see. They are going to work because they have to. I know of a big-time operator around here whose wife drives a school bus because she is short of cash. Just because you are big, that doesn't say that you have got any cash flow." Similarly, Nicole, a resident of the same area, answered, "I did a little survey within the radius of four square sections around our farm and found out that over half of the farm women have off-farm jobs. In most of the cases, the job is to support the farm or provide the food, music lessons, hockey gear, clothes and so on for the family. For most of them, that money was not just being used for frills but was needed cash!"

These comments illustrate the growing trend towards farm women taking off-farm employment. They also reflect the buffering role played by women's off-farm income under depressed economic circumstances. In the same vein, several statistical studies showed that roughly one-third of farm women have off-farm jobs, of whom about thirty percent work full-time.[31] The studies also revealed that many farm women with off-farm jobs—ninety-six percent, according to one Ontario study—allocate part or all of their income to living expenses and farm expenses.[32] For example, a nation-wide survey carried out by the National Farmers' Union showed that forty-three percent of women with off-farm jobs invested fifty percent or more of their off-farm income in the farm.[33] In general, women's off-farm incomes contributed thirty-four percent of the total family income.[34] In analyzing census data, sociologist Pamela Smith found that between 1971 and 1981, a notable increase had taken place in women's off-farm employment in Canada. She also found that an increase had occurred in the number of weeks per year worked off the farm by farm women.[35] The National Farmers' Union survey showed that women employed full-time off the farm still performed seventy-nine percent of the household tasks and eight percent of the farm tasks, with those employed part-time off the farm did eighty-four percent of the household work and almost fifteen percent of the farm work.[36] The studies all agree that "[it] is a well-known fact in our society that the traditional division of labour makes women almost totally responsible for household tasks and childcare. Therefore, with each additional job she takes on, she adds to the absolute number of hours she works and diminishes the amount of 'free time' at her disposal. In the majority of cases where women work in a family enterprise or in the labour force, her total workload is at least double the popular standard of 40 hours per week."[37] In other words, women with off-farm jobs generally carry triple workloads.

While sources of statistical information help us develop a view of farm women's off-farm employment in an aggregate sense, it is more difficult to develop a conception of what women's off-farm employment means in daily life. Interviews with farm women who hold off-farm jobs provide concrete examples of why such jobs are taken, how they are managed alongside other work, and how income from these jobs is allocated. For example, severe cash-flow problems on Cheryl's farm have made it necessary for her to work off the farm. She had been substitute teaching for several years prior to our interview in 1985. She said it was hard to combine working off the farm with raising several small children, but nevertheless, she "put in a request for substituting in all school divisions as far as an hour's drive away." Since no teaching positions were available in the summer and fall of 1985, Cheryl took a job as a waitress. She related, "I was substitute teaching but there wasn't that much work that way. So, when there were positions at [a local hotel-restaurant] I was hired on to help with the banquets. This summer I also worked as a counter girl for a while when they had the barn dances. This was evening work—from eight until one o'clock—and you get to stay and clean things up, so I didn't get home until four or five in the morning. That was difficult. I was too tired! I was really tired." When I spoke to Cheryl again, in the summer of 1987, she told me that, in 1986, she had worked as a library assistant in a nearby school and, in 1987, was lucky to find employment as a substitute teacher again. Cheryl's income from her off-farm jobs was crucial in providing her family with essentials.

In another case, Susan, a farm woman and registered nurse, told me how she allocates her off-farm income. "We bought the farm in 1977. When we moved onto the farm I went to school and took my nursing diploma, because I knew I had to work. I graduated in 1980. My husband, at that time, was also working to supplement the income. The interest rates were terrible. The winter of 1980 to 1981, when we were both working, we were just paying interest, like my whole paycheque. It was discouraging." Between 1980 and 1985, Susan was employed full-time as a registered nurse, and she explained that, by working full-time for five years, she would reach the top of her salary/benefit scale quickly. She told me that her regular and fairly substantial income allowed her husband to take up farming full-time. At present, her income is no longer invested directly in the operation of the farm, yet it continues to contribute to the farm indirectly by meeting family needs. Susan related: "None of my income goes to the farm at all. My income is just for the living for us. The things for the house and the family I can manage on my income. That is how it was always intended to be, except for that first year when we were both working and one of the paycheques would go to the farm." Susan told me that although the farm can now support itself financially, it does not support the family. Her income is therefore crucial in meeting all family needs, which include everything from food to running the family car to paying all family and household bills.

Since our interview, Susan has adopted what she referred to as "part-time" hours—thirty-five hours per week—in order to relieve some of the time pressure. "It was just getting too much," she said. She explained that, despite her off-farm job, the division of labour in the household still falls, to a large extent, along traditional lines. Sometimes her husband helps with meal preparation but Susan continues to do all housecleaning, shopping, laundering, mending, baking, and so on. On average, she works four hours per day on domestic chores, above and beyond her off-farm hours of work. Transporting children to activities consumes an additional hour per day. Susan is also involved in farm work during the growing season but added that she fills in only when needed, usually with combining and going for parts. She mentioned that she would like to be more directly involved in the farm operation, but the family simply cannot do without her off-farm income. She related, "I could probably work maybe a little bit less. Not much less, I don't suppose. I enjoy it but certainly we need it, because that is what we live on. I don't know how we would manage if I didn't work. I can't see how anyone could make it without working off the farm. There is no way!" When asked whether her job gave her a sense of security, she replied, "Oh definitely, because I know that the money is coming and I don't have to worry about paying the bills and nobody is going to take my car away because I can't make the payments."

Like Susan, Linda is a farm woman and registered nurse who works part-time in a nearby hospital. At the time of our interview, Linda told me that the farm still generated enough income to support the family and cover farm expenses but that by renting more land and buying new equipment, she and her husband had incurred a high debt load. Although she asserted that personal satisfaction and not economic necessity is her major reason for working off the farm, she noted the financial contribution her income makes to the farm and family. "We eat my money pretty well. So, I am definitely supporting or helping the farm in that regard. Oh yes, I am! It has definitely helped our banking situation, like the outlook at the bank. It's a thousand dollars a month that isn't coming out of the farm account to pay for clothes and food and birthday presents, and so on. I do with it what is possible and then the farm picks up the slack. I use my money till it is gone and if I run out and there is still, say, something like groceries to be bought, he [her husband] gives me money." Linda mentioned that she does little farm work. Her major contribution to the family and the farm is through the cash income she provides and her domestic work. Like Susan in the previous example, Linda noted how her off-farm job does not alter her domestic responsibilities. When asked whether her job off the farm has changed the division of labour within the household, Linda exclaimed, "No! Not in this house, no! It's just one more job, you see."

As with Linda, Georgina's main contribution to the farm is through her domestic work and the cash income she provides as a full-time teacher. In response to the question whether her income goes directly towards the farm, she said: "At one point yes, but at this point, no." She added that "different farm purchases have been joint purchases." Georgina explained how her income is allocated nowadays. "House purchases I usually make. When we were building the house, it was a joint thing [financially]. We worked together on it. It was sort of fifty-fifty. Furniture, food and groceries, I look after. Clothing as well." With respect to her children's educational and recreational expenses, Georgina noted that "all of that I look after." She added in a speculating tone, "I think we could exist without my working. I think that my husband would find it quite a change though. He would find it quite a drain on his bank book if I were to make all of those purchases out of his bank book. I am not sure that he really realizes just how much we pay for food and clothing." It is clear that Georgina's off-farm income contributes to the farm operation by paying for family and household expenses, thus freeing farm income for re-investment in the farm.

As the economic crisis in agriculture begins to hurt even those farm families whose farm incomes have always been sufficient to support farm and family, women's financial contributions take on a buffering role. Georgina, who worries about the ongoing low grain prices, fully realized the buffering potential of her earnings when she commented, "I guess it is easier for us to feel better about it [low grain prices] because we are a two-income family and my having had a job all these years has certainly been an asset. The paycheque is certainly helpful in the farm operation and, I guess, when there comes to be a crisis, it is not so much of a crisis as it might be otherwise."

The examples I've presented bear witness to the substantial financial contribution of farm women through their off-farm incomes. Not only do they pay for family living expenses and extracurricular activities, but they often also invest their income directly into the farm operation. The current crisis in agriculture has made women's off-farm employment a widespread income-generating strategy.

Off-farm employment is not the only way in which women make financial contributions to their farms. Interviews revealed that many are currently involved in a wide variety of farm-based, income-generating strategies, some of which are reminiscent of cottage industries carried on by farm women in the past.[38] The list is quite extensive. More traditional cottage industries include the production of cream, cottage cheese, vegetables, fruits (both garden fruits and wild fruits), herbs, broiler chickens, turkeys, geese, ducks, eggs, honey, pickles, jams, jellies, fruit juices, preserves, bread, muffins, buns, pies, perogies, clothing and textiles (sewn, woven, knitted, or crocheted articles), wool, and mohair. These products are often marketed locally through such means as roadside stands, "u-picks," farmers' markets, advertisements in local papers, or a network of private customers. Other income-generating activities include the production of greeting cards, signs, pottery, straw sculptures and other handicrafts, bedding plants, woodwork, and cabinetry. A range of services are also provided by women from the farm base, such as income-tax preparation, auditing, and other services using home computers, farm vacations, farm meals, horseback riding and stabling. Others include providing child care, doing contract work as home economists, acting as hunting guides and plucking wild fowl for clients, selling Avon, Tupperware, jewellery, and the like. Some farm women are also involved in the private sale of beef, pork, mutton, and goat milk. Farm-based businesses are an alternative to off-farm employment. Several factors make them more feasible as income-generating strategies. For example, job opportunities and educational facilities to upgrade skills may be lacking. Constraints may be imposed by the need for child care or lack of transportation. Poor road conditions, long travel distances, domestic responsibilities, and involvement in farm production chores may be barriers to taking off-farm jobs as well. Interviews with women who engage in income-generating activities on the farm give insight into what kind of activities are undertaken and why, as well as how income derived from them is allocated. For example, farm woman Colleen of south-central Manitoba raises 300 chickens in the summertime: 150 birds for meat and another 150 for eggs. At one time, Colleen held a teaching position. However, having four babies in a short time curtailed many of her extra-domestic activities. She related, "I sell eggs [and poultry meat]. So, I get a lot of pocket money and kids' money every week out of the chickens. Like, last year I had two thousand dollars from the chickens; eggs and meat sold. And, that is above and beyond what we consume. And, it is cash money! It is something I can do from here [the farm] and there is no time lost really." To Colleen, income generation on the farm is an alternative to off-farm employment. It is easier to combine with housework and child rearing. Although the farm is in sound financial shape, Colleen's extra income contributes to the household budget.

In the case of Tracy, however, the income earned through raising chickens for market is vital to the survival of her and her husband's farm in southwestern Manitoba. The crisis in agriculture has hit their farm particularly hard and Tracy's husband has had to find off-farm employment, which takes him away from the farm for usually one week at a time. As a result, Tracy, with the assistance of her four young children, operates the farm on her own. She also custom-bales straw on neighbouring farms, works off the farm as a school-bus driver, teaches driver education, and raises 400 chickens for sale. Tracy is an example of a growing number of women who employ a variety of income-generating and economizing strategies simultaneously in an effort to rescue the farm from failure. Farm woman Mary Lou has adopted the production of cream as an income-generating activity on her and her husband's farm in southwestern Manitoba. The farm, a mixed operation producing field crops and hogs, needs the extra income to supplement the family's falling farm income. At the time of our interview, Mary Lou had nine milk cows and was selling cream, hoping that, with the extra money, the farm would break even.

As with dairying and poultry raising, small-scale gardening on the side can prove to be profitable for those who need extra cash. A number of women on Manitoba farms have expanded their garden plots to incorporate the growing of vegetables, herbs, and fruits for sale. Some have even cultivated large plots of vegetables and fruits, like strawberries and raspberries, as "u-pick" outlets. For example, Joyce started her corn-selling business in 1985 when she and her husband had to close down the farm's hog operation for lack of investment capital. The loss of an average annual income of $5000, which, as Joyce explained, was all they made raising 600 hogs a year, meant a serious reduction in their overall farm income and a threat to the family's standard of living. In an effort to offset the effects of such a reduction, Joyce planted two acres of corn in 1985 and 1986. The following year, in 1987, she expanded her corn plot to four acres. She explained that the financial returns from marketing her corn help make ends meet on the farm.

In the case of Cheryl, income from the sale of garden produce is also indispensable, since the family was losing the farm and was unable to cope financially without extra cash. She related, "Last year, the money we got selling produce was enough for us to live on financially for the summer. Especially last year, because we had strawberries and they went for five dollars an ice-cream pail and that brought in quite a bit. We made four or five hundred dollars on which we were able to live for the summertime."

In another case, Shirley's income from a farm-based industry is essential in making ends meet as well. She and her husband struggle with start-up debts at a time when prices of grain and cattle, their two main products, are at an all-time low. Her husband has an off-farm job he can not afford to quit. "He has a job and a farm, yet can't support the family," she said. By trade a carpenter and cabinetmaker, Shirley has set up her own shop behind the house, and custom-builds furniture and other articles. At the time of the interview she was not working in the shop, having just given birth. She explained, however, how she normally allocates her income. "If I had my shop going, I paid all the household stuff out of it, and all his [her husband's] money from working out [off the farm] and from the farm went back into the farm. So, now I can't support the household from the shop and I expect it will have to come from the farm." She added, "When I have money in my account and a payment comes up, like with the tractor payments, and my husband doesn't have money in his account, then it comes out of my money to make a payment." This, without a doubt, shows the buffering nature of Shirley's farm-based, income-generating activity, especially under conditions of sudden, acute financial need.

Another farm woman, Carol, has always supplemented family income by carrying out a number of entrepreneurial activities on the farm. Carol explained her income-generating strategy: "I used to do a lot of ceramics, and I sold most of my pieces. But I haven't done it for a while now. I don't like to lay out good money for something to make something. You have to buy the greenware and if you break it, or something happens to it, well, there is your profit gone. I would rather get something for nothing and make it into something." With this philosophy in mind, she began to undertake the following activities:

> I used to go to rummage sales. They'll have clothes or dishes piled up that people have donated and they sell it. I go when the sale is almost over and say: "How much do you want for everything?" I usually get a half-ton truck load of clothing for ten to fifteen dollars. I bring it home and sort out the good from the poor stuff. The poor stuff is good for cleaning rags. I cut all the buttons off and zippers out and put it in bags. I have an outlet where I get fifty cents per pound for the cleaning rags. I sell about two hundred dollars worth a year. And I make quilts too. I take out the better pieces for quilts. I make mitts too, from jeans and old coat linings. They are good working mitts and I sell them for cash too. The kids get the good stuff. Some stuff you burn.

Another business in which Carol got involved, together with her husband, was

> going to auction sales and buying up antiques and other items which we later sold again. We still do that. We buy antique furniture and resell it to [an antique dealer] for a profit. Often, people in the neighbourhood will drop in to see if we have such and such for sale. I also have yard sales. I sell kettles and dishes and I made slippers and three afghans which I sold this summer. Sometimes, I load up my van and go into town. I have the stuff in the van and put up some tables outside. I did it three times this year. I go out to find a good spot where people will stop, especially in town where they go for groceries.

Carol and her husband are also involved in such sidelines as marketing copper salvage from old electric motors. In addition to all this, they cater to hunters. Carol related, "We make some side money by being tour guides to a group of American hunters each year. We get twenty-five dollars per day for that. I've been cleaning geese for these Americans for years. I charge three dollars per goose and I do about ten geese in an hour and a half. I've bought a van for five hundred dollars with my money from cleaning birds. The Americans usually stay for about one week. They stay right here on the farm in the old house. I clean house and cook for them and that makes some money too." Carol told me that, because the farm was never a viable unit without income from other sources, her income from all these entrepreneurial activities was vital in making ends meet. This was especially so when downturns in the farm economy made cash-flow problems worse, as is the case with the current crisis.

Other examples of farm-based businesses were documented in a series of articles published in the *Manitoba Co-operator* from September to November 1986. In these articles, author Susan McLennan described Janet Breemersch's greenhouse and ceramics business, Ruth Wareham's auditing business, Mazo Black's farm-vacations business, Joan Thompson's sign-painting business and cake-decorating sideline, Cathy Wark's wheat weaving, and Marilyn Muller's Christmas-cake enterprise. All these women have been in business for several years. As with other farm women entrepreneurs, these women noted the importance of flexible hours, allowing income-earning activities to take place around child care, homemaking, and farm work. Cathy Wark explained, for example, "You're not making a lot but it's a bonus for me," and added, "I have three kids, so I can stay at home and make a little extra on the side." She earns "enough in a year to cover Christmas and to buy extras that normally we might not buy."[39] Similarly, Ruth Wareham's accounting earns income that is "used for things we otherwise normally wouldn't have from the farm."[40] Joan Thompson's sign painting earned her between $3000 and $4000 dollars in the winter of 1985-86. Most of this money went to supplement the farm income.[41] Marilyn Muller's Christmas-cake business netted about $5000 in 1985. She remarked, "It keeps us in groceries from about the first of October to the middle of January. Plus it pays for Christmas." The business helps keep the family in farming. "It's the only way we can, because the farm certainly isn't paying. . . . You just have to find ways you can stay."[42] Without this income, the family would have to do without many things, she added.

It is evident from all these accounts that women's farm-based businesses provide their farms and families with vital income. While some businesses are reminiscent of cottage industries of the past, many farm women today have come up with new products and services, and have adopted innovative marketing strategies to compete with factory-made products and cope with declining local markets resulting from rural depopulation.

Endnotes

Chapter 1

1. W.L. Morton, *Manitoba: A History* (Toronto: University of Toronto Press, 1967), 85.

2. J.H. Ellis, *The Ministry of Agriculture in Manitoba 1870-1970* (Winnipeg: The Economics and Publications Branch, Manitoba Department of Agriculture, 1971), 403.

3. W.J. Healy, *Women of Red River* (Winnipeg: The Women's Canadian Club, 1923), 99. This work is a compilation of the recollections of women who lived in the Red River Settlement and who were interviewed by members of the Women's Canadian Club in Winnipeg, in 1923.

4. Ibid., 99.

5. It is difficult to establish gender roles in gardening on the basis of literary sources pertaining to this period. W.L. Morton's history of Manitoba (85,87) suggests that men grew the potatoes but neglects to mention who grew the other vegetables. References to garden work after 1870, in the early pioneer period, always mention the involvement of women. Archival materials on women's work on the homestead published by L. Rasmussen, et al. (eds.), *A Harvest Yet to Reap: A History of Prairie Women* (Toronto: The Women's Press, 1976) and H. Robertson (ed.), *Salt of the Earth* (Toronto: James Lorimer and Company, 1974) include numerous autobiographical accounts on vegetable production by women. For example, a woman recalling her first days on the homestead with her husband wrote in 1904, "I remember we were eager for a garden. As soon as a little bit of land was broken we planted peas, beans, radishes, lettuce, etc." (Robertson, *Salt of the Earth*, 28). The film *Great Grand Mother* (Ottawa: National Film Board, 1975), which presents a personal history of pioneer settlement based on the letters, diaries, photographs, and recollections of pioneering grandmothers, gives another good representation of women's work in the garden. Since the early pioneer period represents a continuation of the type of subsistence farming established in the Red River Settlement, women were probably heavily involved in gardening in the Red River era as well.

6. Healy, *Women of Red River*, 150.

7. Ibid., 119.

8. Ibid., 86.

9. B. Kaye, "The Settlers' Grand Difficulty: Haying in the Economy of the Red River Settlement," *Prairie Forum* vol.9, no.1 (1984): 8.

10. Ibid., 11; Kaye was quoting the newspaper *Nor'Wester*.

11. Ibid., 2.

12. Ibid., 6-7.

13. Ibid., 9. Even with small numbers of livestock on each farm, a great deal of hay was needed each winter. One ox needed at least five cart-loads of hay per winter while a horse needed ten. The average family had to procure well over 100 cart-loads. These loads were hauled one at a time, taking up to twenty-four to thirty hours per trip (*Nor'Wester*, May 10, 1864, quoted in Kaye, "Settlers' Grand Difficulty," 9).

14. Healy, *Women of Red River*, 149.

15. Morton, *Manitoba: A History*, 8.

16. Healy, *Women of Red River*, 118.

17. Ibid., 97.

18. Ibid., 110.

19. Ibid., 100.

20. Morton, *Manitoba: A History*, 87.

21. Healy, *Women of Red River*, 147-149.

22. Ibid., 152.

23. Ibid., 153.

24. Ibid., 147.

25. Ibid., 104.

26. Ibid., 146-147.

27. Ibid., 101.

28. Ibid., 100.

29. The sources consulted for the Red River era do not include explicit references to these three activities. Therefore, it is not quite clear to what extent they were carried out.

30. R. Schwartz-Cowan, *More Work for Mother: The Ironies of Household Technology from the Open Hearth to the Microwave* (New York: Basic Books, Inc., 1983), 65. Perhaps the absence of explicit statements about laundering in Healy, *Women of Red River*, indicates that Settlement women washed clothes less often than their later counterparts.

31. K. Strange, *With the West in Her Eyes* (Toronto: George J. Mcleod, 1937), 220-222.

32. The Corrective Collective, *Never Done: Three Centuries of Women's Work in Canada* (Toronto: The Women's Press, 1974), 49.

33. N.L. McClung, *Clearing in the West* (New York: Fleming H. Revell Co, 1935), 33.

34. Healy, *Women of Red River*, 99.

35. Ibid.

36. Corrective Collective, *Never Done*, 33.

37. Healy, *Women of Red River*, 147.

38. Ibid., 96-97.

39. Ibid., 96.

40. Personal communication.

41. Healy, *Women of Red River,* 100.

42. G. Friesen, *The Canadian Prairies: A History* (Toronto: University of Toronto Press, 1984), 162.

43. Rasmussen, et al., *A Harvest Yet to Reap,* 148. Archival accounts and transcribed interviews collected by the editors have been published in this work. I, in turn, draw on these archival accounts and interviews as primary sources of information. References which I make to these primary accounts can be distinguished from references made to the analysis of the editors themselves.

44. *Great Grand Mother.*

45. Ibid.

46. P. Holmes, *It Could Have Been Worse: The Autobiography of a Pioneer Woman* (Toronto: Collins Publishers, 1980), 79-83.

47. Ibid., 100-103.

48. Ibid., 186.

49. M. Ewanchuk, *Spruce, Swamp and Stone: History of the Pioneer Ukrainian Settlements in the Gimli Area* (Winnipeg: Michael Ewanchuk, 1977), 37. This work incorporates previously unpublished archival accounts and transcribed interviews collected by the author. The references which I make to these primary sources of information can be distinguished from references to the analysis presented by Ewanchuk himself.

50. Ibid.

51. Ibid., 32.

52. Robertson, *Salt of the Earth,* 44. This work describes the history of settlement in western Canada using archival accounts. I, in turn, draw on these accounts as primary sources of information. References which I make to these primary accounts can be distinguished from references made to the analysis of the author herself.

53. C.E. Sachs, *The Invisible Farmers: Women in Agricultural Production* (Totowa, N.J.: Rowman and Allenheld, 1983), 13.

54. S.B. Kohl, *Working Together: Women and Family in Southwestern Saskatchewan* (Toronto: Holt, Rinehart and Winston, 1976), 33.

55. Ibid., 34.

56. McClung, *Clearing in the West,* 189.

57. Quoted in Rasmussen, *A Harvest Yet to Reap,* 54.

58. Quoted in Corrective Collective, *Never Done,* 52.

59. Holmes, *It Could Have Been Worse,* 135-141.

Chapter 2

1. Morton, *Manitoba: A History,* 255.

2. Ellis, *Ministry of Agriculture,* 617-618.

3. Morton, *Manitoba: A History*, 156.

4. Ibid., 203-204.

5. Ibid., 276.

6. *History of Minnedosa and Surrounding District* (Publisher unknown, 1958), 147.

7. McClung, *Clearing in the West*, 51.

8. Ibid., 56.

9. Ibid., 127.

10. Morton, *Manitoba: A History*, 161-162.

11. I. Friesen and P. Petkau, *Blumenfeld: Where Land and People Meet* (Winkler: Blumenfeld Historical Committee, 1981), 18. This local history includes a list of Mennonite pioneers settling between 1874 and 1880 and the capital they brought along from Russia.

12. Ibid., 25.

13. Ibid., 140.

14. Morton, *Manitoba: A History*, 309-310.

15. C.A. Dawson and E.R. Younge, *Pioneering in the Prairie Provinces: The Social Side of the Settlement Process*. Canadian Frontiers of Settlement, vol.8, ed. W.A. Mackintosh and W.L.G. Joerg (Toronto: The MacMillan Company of Canada, Ltd., 1940), 88.

16. Friesen, *The Canadian Prairies*, 265.

17. Ewanchuk, *Spruce, Swamp and Stone*, 23.

18. Ibid., 129.

19. Friesen, *The Canadian Prairies*, 267.

20. McClung, *Clearing in the West*, 218.

21. Sachs, *The Invisible Farmers*, 56.

22. Ibid., 46.

23. Friesen, *The Canadian Prairies*, 316.

24. McClung, *Clearing in the West*, 365.

25. Ibid., 364.

26. Strange, *With the West in Her Eyes*, 225.

27. *History of Minnedosa*, 149.

28. Strange, *With the West in Her Eyes*, 220.

29. McClung, *Clearing in the West*, 367-368.

30. Strange, *With the West in her Eyes*, 220-222.

31. Rathwell Historical Committee, *Twixt Hill and Vale: A Story of Rathwell and 0-Surrounding District* (Rathwell: The Rathwell Historical Committee, 1970), 340.

32. *History of Minnedosa*, 149.

33. Robertson, *Salt of the Earth*, 98.

34. The study of J. L'Esperance, *The Widening Sphere: Women in Canada 1870-1940* (Public Archives Canada, 1982), 27, indicated that between 1890 and 1920 there was a shortage of employable women in Canada.

35. McClung, *Clearing in the West,* 366.

36. Cited in Rasmussen, *A Harvest Yet to Reap,* 18.

37. Cowan, *More Work for Mother,* 29-30.

38. Robertson, *Salt of the Earth,* 86.

39. McClung, *Clearing in the West,* 116.

40. Ibid., 128-129.

41. Ibid., 370-371.

42. Friesen, *The Canadian Prairies,* 331.

43. Robertson, *Salt of the Earth,* 102.

44. Rathwell Historical Committee, *Twixt Hill and Vale,* 181.

45. Robertson, *Salt of the Earth,* 68.

46. Ellis, *Ministry of Agriculture,* 404.

47. Cowan, *More Work for Mother,* 12.

48. Ibid., 61-62.

49. Healy, *Women of Red River,* 149.

50. Strange, *With the West in Her Eyes,* 219.

51. Cowan, *More Work for Mother,* 66.

52. McClung, *Clearing in the West,* 178.

53. Ibid.

54. Cowan, *More Work for Mother,* 64.

55. Ibid., 65.

56. Holmes, *It Could Have Been Worse,* 141-143.

57. *History of Minnedosa,* 153; Strange, *With the West in her Eyes,* 222.

58. Cowan, *More Work for Mother,* 65,66.

59. Rathwell Historical Committee, *Twixt Hill and Vale,* 345.

60. Cowan, *More Work for Mother,* 63-64.

Chapter 3

1. Friesen, *The Canadian Prairies,* 310.

2. Robertson, *Salt of the Earth,* 116.

3. Ibid., 98.

4. Ewanchuck, *Spruce, Swamp and Stone,* 261.

5. R. W. Murchie, W. Allen, and J.F. Booth, *Agricultural Progress on the Prairie Frontier,* Canadian Frontiers of Settlement, vol.5, ed. W.A. Mackintosh and W.L.G. Joerg (Toronto: The Macmillan Company of Canada Ltd.), 79,137,138.

6. Morton, *Manitoba: A History,* 210.

7. Ibid., 357.

8. Kohl, *Working Together,* 71.

9. McClung, *Clearing in the West,* 227-228.

10. Robertson, *Salt of the Earth,* 178.

11. Kohl, *Working Together,* 95.

12. Ibid., 85.

13. Rasmussen et al., *A Harvest Yet to Reap,* 42.

14. Ibid., 54.

15. Ibid., 76.

16. Ibid., 72.

17. Holmes, *It Could Have Been Worse,* 97,99.

18. Fisher Branch Historical Society, *A Place of Our Own* (Fisher Branch: Fisher Branch Historical Society, 1982), 179.

19. Ibid., 190.

20. Michael Ewanchuk, *Pioneer Profiles: Ukrainian Settlers in Manitoba* (Winnipeg: Michael Ewanchuk, 1981), 16. This work incorporates previously unpublished archival accounts and transcribed interviews collected by the author. The references I make to these primary sources of information can be distinguished from references to the analysis presented by Ewanchuk himself.

21. *History of Minnedosa,* 153.

22. Ibid., 152-153.

23. Kohl, *Working Together,* 43.

24. Fisher Branch Historical Society, *A Place of Our Own,* 335.

25. Pine River History Committee, *Hardships to Happiness: History Flows from Pine River and District* (Pine River: Pine River History Committee, 1982), 22.

26. Ibid., 114.

27. Fisher Branch Historical Society, *A Place of Our Own,* 280-284.

28. Robertson, *Salt of the Earth,* 62.

29. Pine River History Committee, *Hardships to Happiness,* 152-153.

30. Rapid City Historical Book Society, *Rapid City and District: Our Past for the Future* (Rapid City: Rapid City Historical Book Society, 1978), 161.

31. Ewanchuk, *Pioneer Profiles,* 155.

32. Pine River History Committee, *Hardships to Happiness,* 118.

33. Fisher Branch Historical Society, *A Place of Our Own,* 14.

34. Pine River History Committee, *Hardships to Happiness,* 127.

35. Ewanchuk, *Spruce, Swamp and Stone,* 66.

36. Pine River History Committee, *Hardships to Happiness,* 222.

37. Fisher Branch Historical Society, *A Place of Our Own,* 65.

38. Ibid., 233.

39. Rathwell Historical Committee, *Twixt Hill and Vale,* 333.

40. Riding Mountain and Area History Book Committee, *History of Riding Mountain and Area 1885-1984* (Riding Mountain: The Riding Mountain and Area History Book Committee, 1984), 46.

41. Fisher Branch Historical Society, *A Place of Our Own,* 239.

42. Pine River History Committee, *Hardships to Happiness,* 145.

43. Fisher Branch Historical Society, *A Place of Our Own,* 200.

44. Ewanchuk, *Pioneer Profiles,* 170-171.

45. Rasmussen et al., *A Harvest Yet to Reap,* 43.

46. Ellis, *Ministry of Agriculture,* 513.

47. Ewanchuk, *Spruce, Swamp and Stone,* 66.

48. Ibid., 224-225.

49. Ibid., 255.

50. Ibid., 224.

51. Ewanchuk, *Pioneer Profiles,* 102-104.

52. Rapid City Historical Book Society, *Rapid City and District,* 148.

53. Rathwell Historical Committee, *Twixt Hill and Vale,* 237.

54. Ibid., 114.

55. McClung, *Clearing in the West,* 125.

56. Erickson History Book Committee, *Forest to Field: Centennial History of the Rural Municipality of ClanWilliam and the Village of Erickson, Manitoba, Canada, 1884-1984* (Erickson: History Book Committee, 1984), 47-58.

57. Ellis, *Ministry of Agriculture,* 144.

58. Ibid., 620.

59. Rathwell Historical Committee, *Twixt Hill and Vale,* 323.

60. Robertson, *Salt of the Earth,* 74-77.

61. Rasmussen et al., *A Harvest Yet to Reap,* 52.

62. Erickson History Book Committee, *Forest to Field,* 47-58.

63. Rathwell Historical Committee, *Twixt Hill and Vale,* 103.

64. Ellis, *Ministry of Agriculture,* 273, 512.

65. Rapid City Historical Book Society, *Rapid City and District,* 138.

66. Morton, *Manitoba: A History,* 354-355.

67. Manitoba Agriculture, *Annual Report* (Winnipeg: Department of Agriculture and Immigration, 1917), 28.

68. Manitoba Agriculture, *Annual Report* (Winnipeg: Department of Agriculture and Immigration, 1918), 34.

69. Manitoba Agriculture, *Annual Report* (Winnipeg: Department of Agriculture and Immigration, 1921), 47.

70. Pine River History Committee, *Hardships to Happiness,* 190.

71. Ewanchuk, *Pioneer Profiles,* 57-58.

Chapter 4

1. Ellis, *Ministry of Agriculture,* 603.

2. Friesen, *The Canadian Prairies,* 430-431.

3. Ibid., 432.

4. Manitoba Agriculture, *Manitoba Agriculture Yearbook 1985* (Winnipeg: Department of Agriculture, 1985), 98.

5. Ellis, *Ministry of Agriculture,* 494-495; Manitoba Agriculture, *Manitoba Agriculture Yearbook 1985,* 98.

6. Ruth Berry, "Labour Allocation of Manitoba Farm Women," paper presented at The Canadian Association for Rural Studies, Learned Societies Conference, University of Manitoba, Winnipeg, June 4-7, 1986, p. 19.

7. Nowadays, some farm women use radios to communicate with the workers in the field. This has eased this part of their work of providing transportation.

8. S. Koski, *The Employment Practices of Farm Women* (National Farmers Union, 1982), 31.

9. Council on Rural Development Canada, *Rural Women's Study: Their Work, Their Needs, and Their Role in Rural Development* (Ottawa: Ministry of Supply and Services, 1979), 9 and 78.

10. Berry, "Labour Allocation of Manitoba Farm Women," 8.

11. Cowan, *More Work for Mother,* 85.

12. Ibid., 178.

13. Berry, "Labour Allocation of Manitoba Farm Women," 7.

14. Council on Rural Development Canada, *Rural Women's Study,* 7.

15. Ibid., 74.

16. Berry, "Labour Allocation of Manitoba Farm Women," 17.

17. Koski, *The Employment Practices of Farm Women,* 32.

18. Council on Rural Development Canada, *Rural Women's Study,* 87.

19. Ibid., 88.

20. *Brandon Sun,* 6/1/88.

21. Manitoba Agriculture, "Farm Bankruptcies, Canada, By Province and Enterprise, 1979-1987," Winnipeg: Economics Branch Agricultural Statistics, February 2, 1987.

22. Manitoba Agriculture, "1986 Census Results," Winnipeg: Economics Branch Agricultural Statistics, April 30, 1987.

23. *Brandon Sun,* 29/11/89.

24. Winnipeg *Free Press,* 17/12/84.

25. Council on Rural Development Canada, *Rural Women's Study,* 15.

26. Koski, *The Employment Practices of Farm Women,* 31.

27. Kohl, *Working Together,* 71.

28. Winnipeg *Free Press,* 31/8/85.

29. *Brandon Sun,* 20/11/87.

30. *Brandon Sun,* 9/12/87.

31. Berry, "Labour Allocation of Manitoba Farm Women"; Gisele Ireland, *The Farmer Takes a Wife* (Ontario: Concerned Farm Women, 1983); M. McGhee, *Women in Rural Life—The Changing Scene* (Ontario: Ministry of Agriculture and Food, 1985); Koski, *The Employment Practices of Farm Women,* Council on Rural Development Canada, *Rural Women's Study.*

32. Ireland, *The Farmer Takes a Wife,* 47.

33. Koski, *The Employment Practices of Farm Women,* 25.

34. Ibid., 24.

35. P. Smith, "What Lies Within and Behind Statistics? Trying to Measure Women's Contribution to Canadian Agriculture," in *Growing Strong: Women in Agriculture* (Canadian Advisory Council on the Status of Women, November 1987), 159-160.

36. Koski, *The Employment Practices of Farm Women,* 31.

37. Council on Rural Development Canada, *Rural Women's Study,* 18.

38. Little attention is given to women's farm-based income generation in the literature. The study by the Council on Rural Development Canada, for example, referred to the growing of fruits and vegetables, and the production of family clothing, household articles, food preserves, and crafts as "home production" (Council on Rural Development Canada, *Rural Women's Study,* 16) but did not mention the income-generating potential realized by farm women undertaking these and other pursuits for sale. In another study, Gisele Ireland's survey of farm women in Bruce and Grey counties, Ontario (Ireland, *The Farmer Takes a Wife,* 49), it was noted only that "some of the women [sixteen percent] made extra money by raising chickens and selling eggs, raising rabbits or other fowl, or they were involved in craft production and sales." The marketing of services seems to have been overlooked. Ruth Berry's survey of Manitoba farm families revealed that "only 5 of the [120] families reported that they were involved in a non-agricultural family business such as craft sales or farm vacations" (Berry, "Labour Allocation of Manitoba Farm Women," 10). The survey did not address the marketing of raw and value-added farm products among the enterprises listed above.

39. *Manitoba Co-operator,* 25/9/86.

40. *Manitoba Co-operator,* 30/10/86.

41. *Manitoba Co-operator,* 10/10/86.

42. *Manitoba Co-operator,* 02/10/86.

Bibliography

Aarden, M. *Nou Vraag Ik Je: Een Boek Over Interviewen.* Amsterdam, 1972.

Adamchuk, J. and R. Iwanchuk. *Tent Town, 1898-1979: A History of Minitonas and District.* Minitonas: Community Centre Committee, publication date unknown.

Beck, B. "Cooking Welfare Stew." In *Pathways to Data: Field Methods for Studying Ongoing Organization.* Chicago: Aldine, 1970, pp. 7-29.

Becker, H.S. and B. Geer. "Participant Observation and Interviewing: A Comparison." In *Qualitative Methodology: Firsthand Involvement with the Social World.* Chicago: Aldine, 1970, pp. 133-142.

Berry, R. "Labour Allocation of Manitoba Farm Women." Paper presented at The Canadian Association for Rural Studies, Learned Societies Conference, University of Manitoba, Winnipeg, June 4-7, 1986.

Binnie-Clark, G. *Wheat and Woman.* Toronto: University of Toronto Press, 1979 (1914).

Blok, A. *Antropologische Perspectieven.* Muiderberg: Dick Coutinho, 1977.

Boserup, E. *Women's Role in Economic Development.* London: George Allen and Unwin Ltd., 1970.

Bottomore, T., ed. *A Dictionary of Marxist Thought.* Cambridge: Harvard University Press, 1983.

Brandon Sun, 21/3/1987; 19/9/1987; 20/11/1987; 16/1/1988.

Brandon University. "Working Our Way Out of the Crisis." Proceedings of the Rural Studies Conference held at Brandon University, Brandon, February 27, 1987.

Burton, M.L. and D.R. White. "Sexual Division of Labor in Agriculture." *American Anthropologist* 86, no. 3 (1984): 568-583.

Canadian Council for International Co-operation. "Women and Food Production: Canada and the Third World." Proceedings of an International Conference held at Guelph, Canada, June 15-17, 1984. Ottawa: Canadian Council for International Co-operation, 1984.

Cebotarev, E.A. and F. Shaver. "Women in Agriculture and Rural Societies: Introduction." *Women and Agricultural Production. Resources For Feminist Research* 11, no.1: 1-12, edited by E.A. Cebotarev and F. Shaver, Toronto, 1982.

Cleveland, D.A. "Agricultural Intensification and Women's Work." *American Anthropologist* 87, no.2 (1985): 405-407.

Corrective Collective. *The Never Done: Three Centuries of Women's Work in Canada.* Toronto: The Women's Press, 1974.

Cowan, R. Schwartz. *More Work for Mother: The Ironies of Household Technology from the Open Hearth to the Microwave.* New York: Basic Books, Inc., 1983.

Council on Rural Development Canada. *Rural Women's Study: Their Work, Their Needs, and Their Role in Rural Development.* Ottawa: Ministry of Supply and Services, 1979.

Dawson, C.A. and E.R. Younge. *Pioneering in the Prairie Provinces: The Social Side of the Settlement Process.* Canadian Frontiers of Settlement, vol.8. Edited by W.A. Mackintosh and W.L.G. Joerg. Toronto: The MacMillan Company of Canada, Ltd., 1940.

Department of Indian and Northern Affairs. "An Annotated Bibliography for the Study of Animal Husbandry in the Canadian Prairie West 1880-1925." Department of Indian and Northern Affairs Research Bulletin 77 (January 1978).

Dickman, F.S., ed. *The "Round Table" (Rathwell edition).* Winnipeg: The Wallingford Press Ltd, 1981 (1915).

Doherty, M. "Farm and Off-Farm Work of Alberta Grain Farm Wives and Husbands." Paper presented at The Canadian Association for Rural Studies, Learned Societies Conference, University of Manitoba, Winnipeg, June 4-7, 1986.

Ellis, J.H. *The Ministry of Agriculture in Manitoba 1870-1970.* Winnipeg: The Economics and Publications Branch, Manitoba Department of Agriculture, 1971.

Ember, C. "The Relative Decline in Women's Contribution to Agriculture with Intensification." *American Anthropologist* 85 (1983): 285-304.

Ember, C. "Reply to Cleveland." *American Anthropologist* 87, no. 2: 407-410.

Engels, F. *The Origin of the Family, Private Property, and the State.* New York: Pathfinder Press, 1972 (1877).

Erickson History Book Committee. *Forest to Field: Centennial History of the Rural Municipality of Clan William and the Village of Erickson, Manitoba, Canada, 1884-1984.* Erickson: History Book Committee, 1984.

Estevan History Book Committee. *Estevan 1890-1980.* Vol.1, Estevan: Estevan History Book Committee, 1981.

Ewanchuk, M. *Pioneer Profiles: Ukrainian Settlers in Manitoba.* Winnipeg: Michael Ewanchuk, 1981.

_____. *Spruce, Swamp and Stone: History of the Pioneer Ukrainian Settlements in the Gimli Area.* Winnipeg: Michael Ewanchuk, 1977.

Farm Credit Corporation. *1984 Farm Survey.* Ottawa: Ministry of Supply and Services, 1984.

First National Farm Women's Conference. "The Socio-Economic Status of Farm Women: An Overview"; "The Wife Contributing with her Husband to an Enterprise for Profit"; "Going, going ... Land Use Policy and Agriculture in Canada"; "Old

Macdonald Had a Farm—But Will his Son or Daughter?";"Credit Where Credit Is Due: Women and Farm Credit in Canada"; "The Invisible Pitch Fork: The Portrayal of Farm Women in the Canadian Media." Proceedings of the First National Farm Women's Conference, Ottawa, 1980.

Fisher Branch Historical Society. *A Place of Our Own.* Fisher Branch: Fisher Branch Historical Society, 1982.

Friesen, G. *The Canadian Prairies: A History.* Toronto: University of Toronto Press, 1984.

Friesen I. and P. Petkau. *Blumenfeld: Where Land and People Meet.* Winkler: Blumenfeld Historical Committee, 1981.

Giangrande, C. *Down to Earth: The Crisis in Canadian Farming.* Toronto: Anansi, 1985.

Gillis, V. "A Comparative Analysis of Farm Women's Contribution to the Continuance of the Family Farm in the Maritime Provinces." Paper presented at the Canadian Association for Rural Studies, Learned Societies Conference, University of Manitoba, Winnipeg, June 4-7, 1986.

Harris, M. *The Rise of Anthropological Theory: A History of Theories of Culture.* New York: Harper and Row, 1968.

_____. *Cultural Materialism: The Struggle for a Science of Culture.* New York: Random House, 1979.

Healy, W.J. *Women of Red River.* Winnipeg: The Women's Canadian Club, 1923.

Hedley, M. "A Comparative Study of the Position of Farm Women: New Zealand and Canada." Paper presented at the Canadian Association for Rural Studies, Learned Societies Conference, University of Manitoba, Winnipeg, June 4-7, 1986.

History of Minnedosa and Surrounding District. Publisher unknown, 1958.

Holmes, P. *It Could Have Been Worse: The Autobiography of a Pioneer Woman.* Toronto: Collins Publishers, 1980.

Ireland, G. *The Farmer Takes a Wife.* Ontario: Concerned Farm Women, 1983.

Kaye, B. "The Settlers' Grand Difficulty: Haying in the Economy of the Red River Settlement." *Prairie Forum* 9, no.1 (1984): 1-11.

Kinnear, M. "'Do You Want Your Daughter to Marry a Farmer': Women's Work on the Farm, 1922." In *Canadian Papers in Rural History* 6. Edited by D.H. Akenson. Gananoque, Ontario: Langdale Press, 1988, pp 137-153.

Kohl, S.B. *Working Together: Women and Family in Southwestern Saskatchewan.* Toronto: Holt, Rinehart and Winston, 1976.

Koski, S. *The Employment Practices of Farm Women.* National Farmers Union, 1982.

Kottak, C.P. *Anthropology: The Exploration of Human Diversity.* 3rd ed. New York: Random House, 1982.

L'Esperance, J. *The Widening Sphere: Women in Canada 1870-1940.* Public Archives Canada, 1982.

Leacock, E. "Class, Commodity and the Status of Women." In *Women Cross-Culturally: Change and Challenge.* Edited by R. Rohrlich-Leavitt. The Hague: Mouton, 1975.

Lemaire, T. "Marxistische Antropologie" (unpublished lecture syllabus, 1978).

Luxton, M. *More Than a Labour of Love: Three Generations of Women's Work in the Home.* Toronto: Women's Press, 1980.

Mackintosh, W.A. *Prairie Settlement: The Geographical Setting.* Canadian Frontiers of Settlement, vol. 1. Edited by W.A. Mackintosh and W.L.G. Joerg. Toronto: The Macmillan Company of Canada Ltd., 1934.

Mackintosh, W.A., A.B. Clark, G.A. Elliot and W.W. Swanson. *Economic Problems of the Prairie Provinces.* Canadian Frontiers of Settlement, vol. 4. Edited by W.A. Mackintosh and W.L.G. Joerg. Toronto: The Macmillan Company of Canada Ltd., 1935.

MacPherson, I. "Partners, Not Helpmates: The Role of Women in the Opening of the Rural Prairies." Paper presented at the Canadian Association for Rural Studies, Learned Societies Conference, University of Manitoba, Winnipeg, June 4-7, 1986.

Manitoba Agriculture. *Annual Report.* Winnipeg: Department of Agriculture and Immigration, 1916; 1917; 1918; 1921.

_____. *Manitoba Agriculture Yearbook 1985.* Winnipeg: Department of Agriculture, 1985.

_____. "Farm Bankruptcies, Canada, By Province and Enterprise, 1979-1987." Compiled from data collected by Consumer and Corporate Affairs Canada, Statistics Section. Winnipeg: Economics Branch Agricultural Statistics, February 2, 1987.

_____. "1986 Census Results." Winnipeg: Economics Branch Agricultural Statistics, April 30, 1987.

Manitoba Co-operator, 25/9/1986; 2/10/1986; 10/10/1986; 30/10/1986.

Manitoba Council for International Co-operation. "Women Hold Up Half the Sky." Proceedings of a conference held at Winnipeg, Canada, October 15-16, 1982. Winnipeg: Manitoba Council for International Co-operation.

Manitoba Human Rights Commission. *Out from the Shadows: Bibliography of the History of Women in Manitoba.* Compiled by P. Atnikov. Winnipeg: Manitoba Human Rights Committee, 1975.

Martin, M.K. and B. Voorhies. *Female of the Species.* New York: Columbia University Press, 1975.

McClung, N.L. *Clearing in the West.* New York: Fleming H. Revell Co, 1935.

McGhee, M. *Women in Rural Life—The Changing Scene.* Ontario: Ministry of Agriculture and Food, 1985.

Meillassoux, C. *Maidens, Meal and Money: Capitalism and the Domestic Community.* New York: Cambridge University Press, 1981. Originally published as *Femmes, Greniers et Capitaux,* 1975.

Meulenbelt, A. "De Ekonomie Van De Koesterende Funktie." *Te Elfder Ure* 20, *Feminisme* 1 (1975).

Morton, A.S. and C. Martin. *History of Prairie Settlement and Dominion Lands Policy.* Canadian Frontiers of Settlement, vol. 2. Edited by W.A. Mackintosh and W.L.G. Joerg. Toronto: The Macmillan Company of Canada Ltd., 1938.

Morton, W.L. *Manitoba: A History.* Toronto: University of Toronto Press, 1967.

Mulligan, H. and W. Ryder. *Ghost Towns of Manitoba.* British Columbia: Heritage House, 1985.

Murchie, R.W., W. Allen and J.F. Booth. *Agricultural Progress on the Prairie Frontier.* Canadian Frontiers of Settlement, vol.5. Edited by W.A. Mackintosh and W.L.G. Joerg. Toronto: The Macmillan Company of Canada Ltd., 1936.

National Film Board. *Great Grand Mother.* Ottawa: National Film Board, 1975.

_____. *Settlement of the Western Plains.* Ottawa: National Film Board, 1965.

National Historic Parks and Sites Branch. "A Bibliographic Study of Field Agriculture in the Canadian Prairie West 1870-1940." Research Bulletin no. 46 (February 1977).

Negrych, O. *Toil and Triumph: The Life and Times of Anton and Yevdokia Smermanski, Pioneer Ukrainian Settlers of Manitoba's Interlake.* Publisher unknown, 1981.

Pelto, P. and G. Pelto. *Anthropological Research: The Structure of Inquiry.* 2nd ed. New York: Cambridge University Press, 1978.

Petkau, P. and I. Friesen. *In Search of a Home: The Janzen Family History.* Winnipeg: Irene Friesen-Petkau, 1984.

Petryshyn, J. *Peasants in the Promised Land: Canada and the Ukrainians 1891-1914.* Toronto: James Lorimer and Company, 1985.

Pinchbeck, I. *Women Workers and the Industrial Revolution 1750-1850.* London: Virago, 1981 (1930).

Pine River History Committee. *Hardships to Happiness: History Flows from Pine River and District.* Pine River: Pine River History Committee, 1982.

Pitt, D. *Using Historical Sources in Anthropology and Sociology.* New York: Harper and Row, 1971.

Potrebenko, H. *No Streets of Gold: A Social History of Ukrainians in Alberta.* Vancouver: New Star Books, 1977.

Pritchett, J.P. *Red River Valley 1811-1849.* New York: Russel and Russel, 1970 (1942).

Pugh, T. *Fighting the Farm Crisis.* Saskatoon: Fifth House, 1987.

Rapid City Historical Book Society. *Rapid City and District: Our Past for the Future.* Rapid City: Rapid City Historical Book Society, 1978.

Rasmussen, L., C. Savage and A. Wheeler. *A Harvest Yet to Reap: A History of Prairie Women.* Toronto: The Women's Press, 1976.

Rathwell Historical Committee. *Twixt Hill and Vale: A Story of Rathwell and Surrounding District.* Rathwell: The Rathwell Historical Committee, 1970.

Reiter, R.R. "Men and Women in the South of France: Public and Private Domains." In *Toward an Anthropology of Women.* Edited by R.R. Reiter. New York: Monthly Review Press, 1975.

_____. "Introduction." In *Toward an Anthropology of Women.* Edited by R.R. Reiter. New York: Monthly Review Press, 1975.

Riding Mountain and Area History Book Committee. *History of Riding Mountain and Area 1885-1984.* Riding Mountain: The Riding Mountain and Area History Book Committee, 1984.

Robertson, H. *Grassroots.* Toronto: J. Lewis and Samuel, 1973.

_____. *Salt of the Earth.* Toronto: James Lorimer and Company, 1974.

Ross, L. *Prairie Lives: The Changing Face of Farming.* Toronto: Between The Lines, 1985.

Sachs, C.E. *The Invisible Farmers:Women in Agricultural Production*. Totowa, N.J.: Rowman and Allenheld, 1983.

Schwanke, M. "Concerns of Farm Women." An Information Paper for the Manitoba Action Committee on the Status of Women. 1985.

Selltiz, C. and M. Jahoda, eds. *Research Methods in Social Relations*. New York, 1971.

Shaver, F.M. "Social Science Research on Farm Women: The State of the Art." *Women and Agricultural Production. Resources for Feminist Research* 11, no.1 (March 1982). Edited by E.A. Cebotarev and F.M. Shaver. Toronto.

Smith, P. "Not Enough Hours, Our Accountant Tells Me: Trends in Children's, Women's and Men's Involvement in Canadian Agriculture." Paper presented at the 1985 Annual Meeting, Canadian Agricultural Economics and Farm Management Society, University of Prince Edward Island, Charlottetown.

_____. "What Lies Within and Behind Statistics? Trying to Measure Women's Contribution to Canadian Agriculture." In *Growing Strong: Women in Agriculture*. Canadian Advisory Council on the Status of Women, November, 1987, pp. 123-203.

Stephenson, M., ed. *Women in Canada*. Toronto: New Press, 1973.

Strange, K. *With the West in Her Eyes*. Toronto: George J. Mcleod, 1937.

Sundberg, S. Brooks. "Farm Women on the Canadian Prairie Frontier: The Helpmate Image." In *Rethinking Canada, The Promise of Women's History*. Edited by V. Strong-Boag and A.C. Fellman. Toronto: Copp Clark Pitman Ltd., 1986.

Terray, E. "Historical Materialism and Segmentary Lineage-Based Societies." In *Marxism and "Primitive" Societies: Two Studies by Emmanuel Terray*. New York: Monthly Review Press, 1972. Originally published as *Le Marxisme devant les societes "primitives,"* 1969.

Tiffany, S.W. *Women, Work and Motherhood: The Power of Female Sexuality in the Workplace*. Englewood Cliffs, N.J.: Prentice Hall, 1982.

Univerity of Utah. "An Uncertain Harvest." Salt Lake City: KUED, University of Utah, 1984.

Warkentin, John, ed. *Manitoba Historical Atlas*. Winnipeg: The Historical and Scientific Society of Manitoba, 1970.

Watkins, S. "What Are You Worth? A Study of the Economic Contribution of Eastern Ontario Farm Women to the Family Farm Enterprise." Paper presented at the Second National Farm Women's Conference, Charlottetown, P.E.I., November 21-24, 1985. Women For the Survival of Agriculture.

Weir, T.R., ed. *Manitoba Atlas*. Winnipeg: Surveys and Mapping Branch, Department of Natural Resources, Province of Manitoba, 1983.

Whyte, W.F. "Interviewing in Field Research." In *Human Organization Research: Field Relations and Techniques*. Illinois: Dorsey Press, 1960.

Winnipeg *Free Press*, 17/12/1984; 31/8/1985; 21/3/1987.

Yuzyk, P. *The Ukrainians in Manitoba: A Social History*. Toronto: University of Toronto Press, 1953.